COLD
CALLING
TECHNIQUES

(That Really Work!)

FIFTH EDITION

Also by Stephan Schiffman

Closing Techniques (That Really Work!), 2nd Edition

Power Sales Presentations

Stephan Schiffman's Telesales, 2nd Edition

The 25 Most Common Sales Mistakes (and How to Avoid Them), 2nd Edition

The 25 Most Dangerous Sales Myths (and How to Avoid Them)

The 25 Sales Habits of Highly Successful Salespeople, 2nd Edition

The 25 Sales Skills They Don't Teach at Business School

The 25 Sales Strategies That Will Boost Your Sales Today

COLD CALLING TECHNIQUES

(That Really Work!)

FIFTH EDITION

Stephan Schiffman

Adams Media Corporation
Avon, Massachusetts

Published by
Adams Media, an F+W Publications Company
57 Littlefield Street, Avon, MA 02322. U.S.A.
www.adamsmedia.com

ISBN: 1-58062-856-7

Printed in Canada.

J I H G F E D

Library of Congress Cataloging-in-Publication Data
Schiffman, Stephan.
Cold calling techniques (that really work!) /
Stephan Schiffman.—5th ed.
p.   cm.
ISBN 1-58062-856-7
1. Telephone selling. 2. Telemarketing. I. Title.
HF5438.3.S34   1999
658.85—dc21   98-50876
CIP

This publication is designed to provide accurate and authoritative information with regard to the subject matter covered. It is sold with the understanding that the publisher is not engaged in rendering legal, accounting, or
other professional advice. If legal advice or other expert assistance is
required, the services of a competent professional person should be sought.
— From a *Declaration of Principles* jointly adopted by a Committee of the
American Bar Association and a Committee of Publishers and Associations

Many of the designations used by manufacturers and sellers to distinguish
their products are claimed as trademarks. Where those designations appear in
this book and Adams Media was aware of a trademark claim, the designations
have been printed with initial capital letters.

Front cover photograph by S. Oskar/Stock Imagery.
Rear cover photograph:
The Ira Rosen Studios, South Bellmore, New York

This book is available at quantity discounts for bulk purchases.
For information, call 1-800-872-5627.

This book is
dedicated to AFS.

Contents

Acknowledgments

When this book was first written, its purpose was to give readers insight into the way in which salespeople can effectively make appointments. Since the first edition, I've received hundreds, if not thousands, of letters from people around the world indicating how much the book has helped, how many appointments they've gotten, and how they've improved their success in cold calling.

Since this book is really a compilation of a variety of things that I've learned throughout the years, I want to acknowledge a number of people who have helped me along the way. Specifically, I would like to thank those people who have taken the time to contribute by writing letters of success and of spirit. None of what follows would have been possible without the dedication of Michele Reisner, who has been on our staff for many years and who helped create some of the initial workbooks that are now used by companies throughout the nation. I would also like to thank Brandon Toropov, Steve Bookbinder, Lynne Einleger, Stacia Skinner, George Richardson, Gino Sette, Tina Bradshaw, Carlos Alvarez, Alan Koval, Surendra Sewsankar, Scott Forman, Martha Rios, Anganie Ali, Art Jackson, Raul Nunez, and Andrew Daino, who have also contributed their time and effort.

And, of course, without the support of Jennifer, Daniele, and Anne, none of this could really have taken place.

Introduction

A number of years ago, I decided to take some golf lessons from a pro. (At that point, I should mention, I'd been golfing for quite a while, without ever having taken a lesson.)

During my first lesson, the pro showed me the proper grip for the club. It felt a little awkward, and I told him so. But my teacher assured me that the reason the new grip felt awkward was simple: I had been holding the club incorrectly for many years. Once I got used to the right way of doing things, he assured me, the right way of holding the club would feel just as "natural" as the way I had been holding it. And with that, he demonstrated not only the right grip, but also the right swing and follow-through. It was beautiful.

Well, what he had said sounded logical enough, and it was certainly hard to argue with when he showed off that swing. If only I could get my swing to look as fluid, as graceful, and as powerful as my instructor's!

And yet I had a similar feeling of awkwardness when the golf pro showed me how to stand, where to put my feet, and how to swing. It all felt very uncomfortable. But during my lesson, I swung, as instructed, from that awkward position, and I hit the ball many, many times while the golf pro watched me and offered suggestions.

At the end of the lesson, the pro told me to keep practicing exactly as he'd instructed me. If I did, he promised, the new ways of holding the club, standing, and swinging would soon become second nature.

Well, once I got back on my own, I tried to hold the club, and stand, and swing, as the instructor had told me to. But it still felt strange. I found that when I moved my grip to a "more comfortable" position, it just felt better. And when I stood the way I was used to standing, it just felt better. And when I swung the way I was used to swinging, it just felt better.

So I dropped the lessons and went back to playing golf "my way."

I hit that ball with all my might. I hit it "my way." I hit it so I was "comfortable."

And my average score was 150. (By the way, if you're not a golfer, let me just offer a little bit of background information: the higher the score, the worse the golfer. And 150 is an *extremely* high—that is, bad—score.)

I couldn't understand why nobody wanted to play with me, or why I wasn't getting any better. In fact, I wasted a whole year wondering why my scores were so high.

After a year, I went back to the golf pro. This time, I followed his directions, stuck it out, and practiced the *right* grip, swing, and follow-through over and over and over again, until they became second nature to me. As the golf pro had promised, the correct way of doing things eventually—and the key word here is "eventually"—became "comfortable." And my score dropped!

The thing is, I had to drill the right way of swinging *until* it became comfortable.

Why do I tell you a story about golf in a book about cold calling? Because we all have our "comfortable" ways of doing things: swinging a golf club—following through on the swing—and connecting with people over the telephone.

If we take the time to do what's right—what really works—*over and over again,* until it becomes second nature, it really will feel comfortable. And it really will deliver the results.

If what you're interested in improving is your golf swing, you should talk to a golf pro. If what you're interested in improving is your phone-prospecting technique, you should read this book.

I say that because we've presented the techniques within these two covers to hundreds of thousands of salespeople in virtually every industry, all over the world, and to just about every kind of sales force. If the aim is to get a face-to-face meeting with someone you haven't talked to before, so you can discuss your product or service and how it might fit into that person's operations, this book shows you how to "hold the club," how to "swing," and how to "follow through."

Even if what I suggest that you do in the following pages feels a little awkward at first, I promise you—*it works*. The only reason it feels awkward now is that you're not used to it yet! Once you practice it enough, it won't feel awkward at all.

Fifteen years ago, when I first came up with the idea for this book, I bought a book that was written by someone who had sold *a whole lot* of book proposals to publishers. It outlined a system for selling your book idea to a publisher. It broke the system down into simple steps. I followed the steps, even though some of them felt a little awkward at first. The system worked!

Cold Calling Techniques is now entering its fifth edition. It's been translated into over a dozen languages. It's shown up on bestseller lists. It's sold many hundreds of thousands of copies. It's been cited repeatedly as one of the most important sales-related books ever written.

Now, the reason you're reading this book is, I assume, that you want to set more sales appointments. Well, if that's the case, you're in luck. You are holding in your hands a system written by someone who has set *a whole lot* of sales appointments. This book outlines a system for getting face to face with people to discuss your products and services. It breaks the system down into simple steps. *If you follow the steps—the system will work!*

Once you begin the book, do yourself a favor. Make a commitment to *drill the techniques repeatedly* until they become second nature. Don't waste a year—or more!—of your precious time doing the "same old thing" just because it feels more comfortable than trying something new! *Do what works . . . and stick with it.* And you will certainly see dramatic improvements in your sales prospecting and your overall income level.

I would love to hear your reactions and results once you have implemented the strategies in this book. Please e-mail me at *contactus@dei-sales.com*, or call 1-800-224-2140.

Good luck!

Stephan Schiffman
New York City

CHAPTER 1

Cold Calling
Is Essential

A famous professor at Harvard Business School once asked his students to name the number one reason that businesses do not succeed. He got all kinds of answers, ranging from bad management and bad programs to bad products, poor concepts, and lack of capital. After reading all their answers he stood before his class and told them that the number one reason businesses fail is . . . "lack of sales."

That's it. It's lack of real sales—the work you and I do on the front lines. And if I can't get in the door to see people, I'm not going to sell.

In most selling environments, nothing can happen unless you're able to get that first appointment. No matter how well you sell, if you can't get in the door, if you cannot get an appointment to see somebody, you're not going to sell.

To become a successful salesperson, you have to develop a solid base of prospects. This base will only remain solid if you continue to prospect successfully—and the cold call plays a large part in successful prospecting. Cold calling is the best and most economical way for you to develop prospects on an ongoing basis. This book is devoted to helping you get in front of your prospects in the most efficient, profitable way—and to overcome your number one competitor.

Your Biggest Competitor

Who is your number one competitor? Interestingly enough, you can name every company in your business—and you'll be wrong. No matter what company you mention, I'll tell you you're wrong. You could tell me that you are your own competitor. You'd be wrong again. You could say to me that your energy level is your competition. Wrong.

Your number one competitor today is the *status quo*. The *status quo* is what people are doing right now. If you understand that, you're going to be successful. It's rare that we're really up against a competitor—we're usually up against the incumbent, the status quo. Remember, most of your potential customers are happy with what they've got—otherwise, they would be calling you!

Once when I was doing a training session I stated that your number one competitor is the status quo. A sales rep raised his hand and said, "Steve, I've never heard of that company. Who's Status Quo?" Don't get sidetracked. Remember: you're up against *what the prospect is already doing.*

Where Sales Come From

Now, I'm going to discuss something that upsets many salespeople. The fact of the matter is you're going to get one-third of all your sales no matter what you do. Let me repeat that: *You'll get one-third of all your sales no matter what you do.*

In the United States nearly 1,000 copiers are sold every single hour of every single day. It's estimated that nearly 2,000 cellular numbers are installed in the United States every hour.

What do numbers like that tell you about sales? They should tell you that there are people who need your product . . . just like you need to go to the supermarket to buy milk. That's a consumer-driven sale.

In fact, you and I have seen people who shouldn't be allowed to walk the streets without a leash who still make sales. The reason people like that are able to make a living is that their sales *are* based on needs for those consumer-driven products. Eventually something breaks; eventually you're going to need a new car; eventually you're going to need more lettuce; eventually you're going to buy a new television. Successful salespeople understand that they'll get one-third of their sales no matter what, simply because they knock on enough doors. But is that enough?

The Sales You'll Never Get

Then there's one-third of your sales that you're *not* going to get. For whatever reason, no matter what you do, you're just not going to get the last one-third of your sales. Sometimes it's because the other guy, the other salesperson, gets it. Sometimes there are internal changes at the target company that you can't control. Either way, you're not getting the business.

The Sales That Are Up for Grabs

The last one-third is up for grabs. That's what we're going to discuss here. We'll show you how to develop your competitive edge, get more appointments, and get more of that last one-third, which is where the good salespeople separate themselves from the mediocre salespeople.

The interesting thing is that plenty of salespeople make their living by simply accepting the first one-third. That's really more of an order-taking situation.

In fact, there's a guy in Times Square who sells a little wallet-like card case. He simply stands there and says, "Wanna buy, wanna buy, wanna buy, wanna buy, wanna buy, wanna buy, wanna buy, wanna buy?" You get the idea. That's all he does!

That tells you something about the entire sales process. If you see enough people, you will *eventually* make a sale. In fact, as we mentioned earlier, you're going to make a certain number of sales no matter what you do. If you knock on enough doors, it doesn't make any difference what you do, eventually you're going to get a sale.

Suppose I went to the busiest street corner nearest my office (it happens to be Times Square), and I simply put out my hand. Do you think anybody would put money in my hand? Of course, eventually someone's going to do that. That's my first third. Now if I held out a cup, do you think I might make more money? Of course. If I add a cup and a bell, *bing-bing-bing-bing,* would more people give me money? Of course. Add a cup, a bell, *bing-bing-bing-bing,* and a sign, "Please help me." Would more people give me money then? Absolutely.

The point, again, is that you'll eventually make a sale if you see enough people. But this story illustrates that it's equally important to make the most of the opportunity. It's not enough to just see people or talk to people on the phone. You have to use the right tools.

The other day I was walking in Manhattan near our office and I noticed a bank with a table right outside displaying a sign that read, "SIGN UP FOR PC BANKING." Three bank employees simply approached every single person who walked past them. I went up to one of them and asked, "How did you do?" They said, "It was incredible today." In the last two hours they had signed up 200 people for their PC banking program—people who had simply walked past the building.

One of the great telecommunications giants in the country today started many years ago by setting up tables outside of major office buildings with a sign that simply said, "SAVE MONEY ON LONG DISTANCE." And people would sign up.

You and I could make sales that way. Simply going after the first third, and doing nothing else, however, is *not* the way to build a successful sales career. I doubt even that telecom giant could survive today if all they had were a couple of tables and a few homemade signs!

Timing Is Everything

When we begin to look closely at the prospecting process, we can see why the concept of time is so important. I know that it takes me about eight weeks from the time I first sit down and talk to a prospective client to the time I make a sale. So let's play this out and see how it works. If I sat down with you on January 1st, I'd know that, if we decide to do business together, I'm going to see a sale not in February, but in March—say, on March 1st. January 1st to March 1st. If my sales cycle is 18 weeks, it's going to take me that much longer. The sale will be closer to May.

If, on January 1st, I'm busy because it's a holiday and I don't call anybody, and on January 2nd I don't call anybody because I'm doing something else, I've pushed out the date when I can expect to see a sale. Say I don't prospect on January 3rd, 4th, 5th, 6th, 7th, 8th, 9th, or 10th. Now instead of March 1st, it's going to be March 2nd, 3rd, 4th, 5th, 6th, etc. I think you get the point.

Think about it like this: When you get paid for a sale, when did you really earn that money? Depending on your sales cycle, it could have been as long as three months or even a year ago. If you didn't do some kind of prospecting a year ago, the odds are that you would not see any income now. If you look at it this way, what you suddenly realize is that the appointments that you generate *today* are what create the prospects you meet, which ultimately give you your sale at the end of your sales cycle.

Now that you've read about how important time is, you're probably jumping out of your chair saying to yourself "I've got to get started!" Please remember to finish the whole book before you try to implement the program.

Reducing the Sales Cycle

A couple of weeks ago I went on a sales call. It was a good sales call. How do I know it was good? Because while I was there, I set up an appointment to come back. *By setting the next appointment on my first appointment, rather than waiting until later, I accelerated my sales cycle by three to five weeks.*

Let me explain. Typically, on an appointment, a salesperson will tend to say to the prospect, "I'll call you in a week." Now we've added at least a week to the sales cycle. Then what happens? We might not get the person on the phone that next week. Now we have to wait. Finally, we get the person on the phone, setting an appointment for perhaps two to three weeks later.

By setting the next appointment *during the first one*, we can save all this wasted time. We really can reduce the sales cycle by three to five weeks!

Gerbil Selling

Let me share another story. Recently a sales call of mine went very well. The presentation was great! Since the presentation had gone so well, I asked for the sale:

Steve: It makes sense to me. What do you think?

Prospect: We can't do it now.

Steve: Why not?

Prospect: I gotta talk to my boss.

Steve: (Because time is so important) Okay. Let's go see him now.

Prospect: Well, we can't do that. I need a week.

Steve: I'll come back in a week.

Prospect: Nope, no good. I'll call you.

Steve: No, I'll call you.

Prospect: I'll call you.

Steve: I'll call you.

Prospect: Steve, trust me. I will get back to you. Honestly, I'll get back to you.

Steve: Okay.

There was nothing else I could do. One week went by, then two. I didn't hear from him. Three, 4, 5, 6, 7, 8, 9, 10, 11, 12, 13, 14, 15, 16, 17, 18, 19, 20 . . . It's now, I don't know, maybe 98 weeks later and I still haven't heard from him. What do you think my chances are of making the sale? Virtually zero. The point is that time is of the essence. The longer the sale goes out of the normal cycle, the less likely it is to happen.

Does this next example sound like a normal sales cycle? A woman in Rockville, Maryland, once told me she went on 37 appointments to the same contact at one company. The same person, 37 times, and she still hadn't made the sale! Would you do that? Of course not! What could the two of you possibly talk about on the 37th visit that hadn't already been covered on the first 36? Isn't that a waste of time?

Years ago I went on a sales call, and the person I was dealing with knew that I usually only go back three times. I typically either close on my third call or conclude that the sale isn't going to happen right now. On the third call my contact at this company said: "I know you usually only come back three times. Would you come back one more time? It's going to be worth a half million dollars to you." I said I'd come back.

When I went on that fourth meeting, the prospect said to me again: "This is really great. Would you come back one more time?" I came back one more time. At the end of the next meeting, he said to me: "This is really great. Would you come back one more time?" I came back one more time. And, of course, when the same thing happened at the end of that meeting I got suspicious. So I asked: "What am I coming back for?" He replied, "Well, I want you to meet Mr. Big. He's going to give you a million dollar deal, not five hundred thousand." One million dollars!

Of course, I came back again. He asked again: "Would you come back one more time? I want you to meet some more people." I went back again.

In fact, I went back *11 different times* for this company. What do you think happened the eleventh time? At the end of the eleventh meeting, they said to me: "Steve, we're not going to buy."

What did they do to me? What they did was convince me, against my usual practice, to run around in circles and waste a lot of time.

I call that gerbil salesmanship. At home, my kids have two gerbils. One runs around continuously in the miniature Ferris wheel in the little cage. He's a very busy gerbil. In fact, he's absolutely exhausted at the end of the day. Gerbil salespeople run around in circles all day but get nowhere.

The Open Door

At my company we have an open door policy. Anyone who wants an appointment with me can get one. In fact, I try not to screen phone calls. I think it's important to meet each and every salesperson who wants to talk to me. I'm eager to meet them and understand what they have to sell. To me it's foolish for executives not to see salespeople from time to time. Why not keep up-to-date with what's going on in their fields? Granted, not everyone thinks that way. (Wouldn't our jobs be easier if everyone did?)

Whether your prospects have an open door policy or not—your goal has to be to *get the appointment*. To learn why that goal is so important, read on.

CHAPTER 2

By the Numbers

When I started my company nearly 20 years ago, I did not know how to get appointments. I sat in the office waiting for the phone to ring because I was convinced that people would call me. I hired a secretary and an associate to help me field the calls. We sat there saying to ourselves, "We have an ideal situation."

We knew exactly what it was we were going to sell. We knew that people needed it (there's the word "need" again) and we thought that all we had to do was send out enough announcements about our business, and people would start calling us.

How naive was that? I would be glad to send you some of the 10,000 brochures and 10,000 pens with my name and telephone number on it that I still have. Circulating them didn't get people to call us!

I learned very quickly that if I was not able to get appointments, I was not going to be successful. The key to successful selling has to be getting appointments, but most salespeople don't realize that. Sixty-five percent of success, I've learned, is finding people and telling them what you do.

The A=P=S Formula

There's a formula that's more important to successful salespeople than any other: A=P=S. In other words, Appointments give you Prospects give you Sales. If you have no new appointments today, what's your chance of getting a new prospect? It's nonexistent. If you have no new prospects, what's your chance of making a sale? That, too, is nonexistent.

The real question is, how many appointments do you need to generate one real prospect? (A prospect is someone who consciously agrees to move through the sales process with you. We'll look at this definition more closely in Chapter 3.) Your appointment base is always going to be larger than your prospect base, which is going to be larger than your sales base. It's like a pyramid, with your appointments forming the base, your prospects forming the middle, and your final sales at the top.

For example, suppose that you don't make any new appointments today. You're not going to generate a new prospect. That means that, approximately eight weeks from now, you'll see no new sales. Now, you can argue with me and say, "People will call me." But that's not what we're talking about. We've already established that's going to happen; those are consumer-driven sales. We're talking now about how to get at that *last* third of all possible sales.

A=P=S. Or, if you prefer, zero A=zero P=zero S. No appointments, no prospects, no sales.

Know Your Numbers

How many appointments do you need to get your prospects? How many dials on the phone does it take to get those appointments? If you don't know those numbers, how can you know whether your sales approach is working?

In my case, I know I need one appointment a day, or five new appointments a week. In order to do that, I have to call 15 people each day. Fifteen times five gives me 75. Over five days, I dial 75 people, I generate five new appointments, which ultimately gives me my one sale every single week. And that's the objective. That ties into the question I asked you before. If you don't know the numbers you need to reach your goal, you're probably not going to get there.

How many cold calls do you make each day? Do you know? If so, *why* do you make that number of calls? Are they true cold calls, or are they calls you've been repeating by calling the same people over and over again?

Every single day that I'm not in front of a group, I still pick up the phone 15 times; that is, I still make 15 calls. That's 15 new people I haven't spoken to before.

Even on busy days I still try to find a way to make those 15 calls. On those days when I cannot reach anybody during normal business hours, I call 15 new people starting at 7:00 A.M. I know the odds are that I will not reach people that early. But I also know that I will have 15 messages out there, and at least one of those people will call me back.

Typically, though, I call 15 people a day, and I actually speak to seven of those people. For every seven people I speak to, I set up one new appointment. As a rule, I do that five days a week, so at the end of the week, I have five new appointments. That's five people that I have not met with before.

Now here's a trick question. If I make five new appointments this week, as I always do, how many total appointments will I have *next* week?

Do you know the number? It's eight. Why is it eight? Because I know for every five new appointments, I'm going back to three more for follow-through appointments.

If you say to me that you have five appointments for this week, but you have no follow-through appointments, then the odds are you did not have five appointments *last* week. My total number of appointments (eight) is very important. My closing ratio happens to be that for every eight appointments, I make one sale. This means that I will bring in something in the neighborhood of 50 new accounts a year.

Why is that important? Well, suppose I didn't make those 15 calls a day. What would happen? I'd be out of business! The 15 calls that I make every day give me the 50 new accounts a year. In other words, the 15 calls drive the 50 sales. Cold calling is a numbers game (or, to be more precise, a ratios game). And this particular game *drives your sales.*

Now, I'll go back to my initial question. How many calls do you make each day? Is it giving you the number of appointments that you require in order to be successful? I know that I must get one new appointment a day, and that I have to make 15 calls, and speak to seven people, to set up that one new appointment. I do that five days a week. Those are my numbers. How many appointments do *you* require to be successful? If you must make five new appointments a week, are you getting them? If you require ten new appointments a week, are you getting them? More important, how did you settle on the numbers you're working with?

Here's a simple question. Do you know the mileage of your car? Most people can tell me automatically that their car has X amount of miles on it. They know how many miles per gallon they get in that car. Yet if I ask the same person, "Do you know how many appointments you went on last week?" they often don't know. Which figure matters more to your yearly income?

You need to know your numbers and understand your ratios. I'm going to show you how increasing your sales can be as simple as getting one or two more appointments a week. You are not going to get twenty more appointments a day. That's unrealistic. But if you get *one* more appointment a day, consistently your sales are going to increase.

A lot of salespeople don't know where their numbers came from. What they do just evolved; it just kind of happened. That's not the way to take control of your career. Only use numbers that give you the actual number of sales and/or appointments you must generate each and every day, week, month, and year.

Numbers from the Real World

Let me give you a series of numbers that I think are important: 293→149→49→83→10.

Now these are actual sales numbers. Let me tell you what they represent. In this particular case, this salesperson picked up the phone 293 times during a 10-week period. During that time, he spoke to 149 people and actually set up 49 first appointments. The 83 represents the total number of sales visits. Of course, that's higher than the number of first appointments because it includes repeat or follow-through visits. Ten represents the number of sales. When you analyze these numbers, what you start to understand is that the salesperson made one sale and went on an average of 8.3 appointments each week for 10 weeks.

This person actually set up about five appointments every week for 10 weeks and made about 30 dials a week, or six dials a day every day, for 10 weeks. Not exactly a major blowout in terms of numbers, but successful nonetheless. Why? Because this person *understood his numbers*. His goal was a new sale a week; he monitored his numbers and hit the goal.

I have somebody working for me who made $68,000 his first year with me; he picked up the phone 2,448 times. Now that may seem like a lot to you, but when you really think about it, it's only 10 calls a day (assuming a 250-day working year). In other words, if I promised you that if you picked up the phone 10 times a day you would definitely make $68,000, would you do it? Of course you would. The fact is, every single time you pick up the phone you're getting *closer to a yes*. If you understand that concept, you'll be successful in sales.

Avoiding Peaks and Valleys

Another reason prospecting and getting appointments is so important has to do with the peaks and valleys, the ups and downs that so many salespeople experience. What most of them don't realize is that *there's no need to have peaks and valleys!*

Let's look at why these peaks and valleys occur. Think about the ratios we just discussed. Think about the number of noes that you get in relation to each sale. You'll realize that, when you make a sale, you actually lose prospects!

Let's say, for argument's sake, that you're working on 20 prospects. These are 20 people whom you've met, and you're going back to meet them. They're working with you. Let's say your closing ratio is one out of five. When you make a sale within that group of 20, what actually happens is that you've made one sale and four people have said no. That's one sale out of five prospects, which means you now have only 15 prospects (even though 19 still *seem* to be active). Now, if you make another sale from these 15 prospects, you'll only have ten prospects left. If you make another sale, you'll have five prospects left. Soon you'll have nothing left.

Salespeople often repeat the process I just described. And in doing that they *create* peaks and valleys. They don't replenish prospects soon enough. They have highs and lows because they work their way through their prospects. They make their four or five sales out of the 20 prospects that they had, *without replenishing that base of prospects.*

In order to avoid these peaks and valleys, we have to replenish or re-establish that base constantly. How long does that take? Depending on your sales cycle it could be 8, 10, or 12 weeks, 90 days, or it could be a year. Whatever time frame your process demands, when you get a big sale (or even a little one), you have to check for peaks and valleys and replenish your prospect base.

Salespeople talk about the "big sale" all the time. They say, "Steve, I had the greatest month I ever had last month." I ask, "What did you do the month before?" "Well, it wasn't so good." "What are you doing the month after?" "It doesn't look so good." To really understand how well their sales are going, they need to average their sales over that three-month period. When they do, their sales numbers are probably going to look suspiciously like the one-third that they would have gotten anyway—unless they've continuously worked on developing new prospects.

Prospecting and the Sales Cycle

The need for "perpetual" sales prospecting becomes even more obvious if you consider how far your sales efforts take place in advance of your sales revenues. For example, if it takes 60 days to generate a sale, 30 days to implement the program, 30 days to use the service, 30 days to bill, and 30 days to get paid, that means *six months* pass between the start of the process and when you actually see the first dollar. You may think you're making sales today, but the sale you made today came from the work you did yesterday. Again, Appointments = Prospects = Sales.

Recently I was working with a software company that had had a tremendous year. I talked to the president of the company about what had happened that year. The conversation went like this:

Steve: What happened last year?

Company President: Well, from January to June we had a tremendous year. We had 15 people call us and we got 15 major accounts. It was just a great year.

Steve: And what happened after that?

Company President: Well, people stopped calling!

Steve: So what did you do?

Company President: Well, we uh . . . (Silence.)

Steve: So what did you do?

Company President: Well, you know, we, uh, we started
thinking about what to do.

Because their sales cycle takes nearly a year, their sales
have now plummeted, and they are in real danger of going
under. And the fact is, that downturn didn't have to happen.

Keep on Prospecting!

Even if you have a successful week, a successful month, or a
successful year, that doesn't mean you should ever stop
prospecting. One of the biggest mistakes that we make is we
convince ourselves that we don't have to prospect on a regular
basis. We get happy and complacent with our existing business
and we think we don't have to seek new business.

Prospect constantly, every single day.

I learned the importance of prospecting some years
ago when my business got very busy. We got an assignment
in August that sidetracked everyone in the organization.
We stopped prospecting for about two months. It was
incredible the amount of work that we had to do on that
assignment, and every trainer and every staff person was
involved. You know the rest of the story, don't you? You
guessed it: in October our sales plummeted. It was
December before it started to build up again, but, of course,
December is a light month, and it wasn't until January that
we saw the light at the end of the tunnel. That was a

harrowing few months; I've promised myself that we'll never go through that again.

A number of years ago my number one salesperson, someone who's been with me for years, got very sick. I was extremely worried about her, as we all were. Although she passed the crisis safely, she had to stay in the hospital for a number of weeks. When I was sure the worst was over, I became concerned about her appointments—because there weren't any! So there I was in the hospital saying, "Sit up, sit up." She said, "Well, I can't—I've got this thing in my nose and . . ." I said, "You're fine. You can talk on the phone. Make the calls; you have to make calls now."

Maybe that sounds harsh. Why did I do that? Because I knew that her sales would drop in eight weeks if she didn't make those calls. It's a terrible story, but it's true. Without her calls, her business was going to suffer a crisis, too, and I knew she didn't need that.

The key, then, is to keep prospecting on a regular basis. Making the sale is important, but it's *not* as important as managing your prospects. And the key to that is to replenish your base of prospects with new appointments. It's worth repeating. If you don't have enough appointments, you're not going to get enough prospects. If you don't get enough prospects, you're not going get enough sales, and you're not going to be in business. A=P=S!

If you keep this concept in mind, and act on it, you should be able to avoid the peaks and valleys.

The Value of a "No"

Earlier in this chapter I asked you, "How many appointments do you need each week?" Then I asked, "How many calls do you need to make each day to get that number of appointments?" *If you don't know these numbers, you're not going to be successful.*

It can be frustrating—but you're going to get plenty of "no" answers when you make these calls. Ready for a surprise? You really shouldn't be too concerned about the number of "no" answers you're getting. Because if you're not hearing "no," you're not making sales. This addresses a basic criticism—that my cold calling approach doesn't work 100 percent of the time. It doesn't! It's not designed to work 100 percent of the time. It's designed to give you a *competitive edge.* Everything I'm sharing with you is designed to help you improve your numbers over where you are today. That's what this book is all about.

So realize that there is a ratio of "no" answers to "yes" answers. A typical ratio would look like this: You're going to make 20 calls, speak to five people, and set up one appointment. Or you're going to see 20 people, make 5 presentations, and make 1 sale. What's important to understand about that 20, five, and one ratio is that in the process of doing that, you're going to hear "no" 19 times. In other words, for every appointment or sale you get, you have to collect 19 "no" answers.

My company does a lot of work with life insurance companies and HMOs around the United States. In fact, we train life insurance agents around the world. When we work with a brand-new life insurance agent, somebody who's just been hired, we will give that person a chart with 250 boxes on it.

Every single time that person talks to someone about life insurance and hears, "No, I don't want to buy," or "No, I'm not interested," the salesperson puts an X in the box. When the chart is full, that is, when 250 people have said no, we give the person $1,000. Why can we do that? Well, if you stop to figure it out, you'll realize that in the process of getting 250 "no" answers, that salesperson will probably generate $10,000 in sales. In other words, we can afford to pay out $4 for every "no," because we know we're going to make it back.

It's important to understand that *every time someone says no, you're getting closer to a yes.*

Did You Hit Your "No" Quota Last Week?

Did you get enough "no" answers last week? Did you hear "no" enough times to generate a sale? If you don't know the answer, my guess is you don't know your ratios yet. If you're not getting enough "no" answers, you're not getting out there enough.

I meet with many different sales forces throughout the United States. Sometimes sales managers say to me, "Steve, we had a great week last week. Nobody turned us down!" I know they were either on vacation or they weren't selling at all. Learn to count the "no" answers!

There's a great insurance brokerage firm I know of, where the owner of the company literally walks around and says, "How many 'no' answers did you get?" And if a salesperson ever says, "Man, I had a rough day, everyone was turning me down," the owner says, "That's great! We're going to make a sale."

Interestingly enough, if you understand this concept, and know the ratios, you can predict *how long* it will take you to reach a certain level of sales. You can make a chart that shows that it's going to take you, let's say, three months to generate the "no" answers you need to reach the level you've identified.

We had a new representative in Chicago a while back who was not doing well his first few months on the job. As a manager, I knew that he had to get a certain number of "no" responses in order to be successful. On day, he called me and told me that he was discouraged because he hadn't yet closed a sale, and he was thinking of leaving the company. I asked what his calling numbers were; then I said, "Based upon what you're telling me, right now you need two more 'no' answers."

He asked what I meant. I said, "If you make enough calls to get two more "no" answers, you're going to have enough, and you're going to make a sale." And that is exactly what happened—he stuck with it and closed his first sale on his 101st day with our company.

Five Ways to Double Your Income

Let me give you some more examples of numbers and ratios so you can have a feeling of what to expect.

One sales force I worked with in New York picked up the phone 606 times, spoke to 315 people, and set up 152 appointments.

Here's another example. This person was selling advertising in the Chicago area: 736 dials, spoke to 358 people, and set up 138 appointments.

Here's another from a company in Los Angeles: made 203 dials, spoke to 99 people, and set up 66 brand-new appointments.

Here's another from a company in Florida: made 589 dials, spoke to 213 people, and set up 102 appointments.

These numbers are from across the country, so don't say, "Well, this program won't work here in (fill in the blank)," because it will!

Let me explain why these numbers are so important. There are five ways in which you and I can double our income, based on what we do with these numbers.

1. Double the Number of Calls

The first way to double your income is to simply double the number of calls you make. In all the seminars that I conduct, and I do about 150 to 200 seminars a year, I ask people if they can double the number of calls they make. Every once in a while I get somebody who says, "Yes, I think I could double the number of calls." "Well, if that's the case," I imme-diately say, "then the seminar is over! There's no need for you to continue." If in fact you can double the number of calls you make every day, then just do it. You don't need *me* to tell you what to do. Double your number, and you'll get more sales. For most people, unfortunately, that's probably not a realistic option.

2. Get Through More Often

A second way to double your income is simply to get through to more people. For example, on a typical day, I call 15 people and speak to seven of them. Now, getting through to 14 people might be tough. But if I got through to eight people a day, would it change anything? Well, one more person a day means over 200 more people a year. That's a big number. Think about how a similar change would affect your numbers.

3. Get More Appointments

A third way to double your income is simply to get more appointments. In other words, instead of speaking to seven people and getting one appointment every day, I could get two appointments, or even 1.2 appointments. As long as I increase that ratio over time, I'm going to be more successful. If I got one more appointment a day, the amount of additional income I could generate would be incredible! But even a smaller increase could make a dramatic difference. This book will show you how to get more appointments from the people you're speaking to on the phone.

4. Close More Sales

A fourth way to increase my income is to get more sales from my appointments. My closing ratio is one out of eight.

For every eight appointments, I'm going to make a sale. What if I could improve that ratio? What if I could go to 6-to-1 or even 4-to-1? Again, a dramatic improvement. Of course, I'd have to see the same number of people while I was improving that ratio.

5. Generate More Dollars Per Sale

Finally, I could go down to my last number, my 50 new accounts, and simply raise the stakes. If I could just get twice as many dollars out of each sale, I could (theoretically at least) double my income.

That idea isn't quite as outlandish as it may sound. A woman from a major oil company called my office at 10:00 on a Friday night to buy 10 copies of an earlier edition of this book. I said to myself, "Here's a woman calling me at 10:00 on a Friday night. She probably doesn't have a life." Of course, it wasn't long before I thought, "Here I am at 10:00 on Friday night answering the phone. I must not have a life either!" In any event, I asked her, "Why are you calling this late on a Friday night?" She said, "Steve, I'm calling you because we have 10 distributors down here in the Virginia area and we want them to make more appointments. We thought your book would help." I said, "You know something, I've got a great idea. Why don't we get together in person?" I turned an $80 book sale into a $250,000 program simply by asking the question, "What is it you're trying to accomplish?"

The point is that if I can increase the average dollar amount per sale, I'm going to be more successful and sometimes there are opportunities to do just that.

So there they are—five ways I can increase my income: double the number of calls, do a better job of getting through, do a better job of getting the appointment in the first place, do a better job of closing, and finally, make higher-dollar sales.

Just One More Call a Day

If you watch sports, you know the difference between winning and losing is often one stroke, one run, or even one fraction of a second. You don't have to win by a mile. You just have to win. To be number one, to be the best, or even to just make a dramatically better living doesn't require that you get 1,000 more points. Just one more point is often the margin of victory. You don't need 1,000 more appointments a day. You may just need one.

Years ago I did a program for a pharmaceutical company. Their top representative was a young man who had beat out 650 other reps for the top spot in the organization. The senior managers had asked me as part of my speech to ask this particular salesperson what he did that made him so special. He was not briefed on this ahead of time, and he didn't know the question was coming. I'll never forget this, because he was a big guy—about 6'4"—and I walked over and asked him to stand. Then I looked up at him and said, "Jim, just out of curiosity, how did you become number one?" He said, "I made one more call at the end of the day." And I said, "What do you mean?" I was just flabbergasted. I thought he would give me a whole elaborate story about what he did. What he said was very simple. He said he decided he wanted to be number one in the country. He normally made all of his prospecting calls in the morning. Every single day, just when he was ready to leave the office, no matter what time it was, whether it was five o'clock, six o'clock, seven o'clock, or eight o'clock, he sat down at his desk with his coat on and he called and spoke to one more person.

That's success. That's what it takes. You don't need to get a thousand more people on the phone. You may just need to get one more person on the phone every day.

Let's look at this more closely. Take a look at the set of numbers that I gave you before: 149 conversations with new people, 49 first appointments, 83 total appointments, and 10 sales. If that salesperson had merely spoken to one more person a day, gotten one more appointment a day, made one more sale a day or a week, or had increased any one of those numbers by one, he would have increased his income substantially.

If you want to be successful in sales, you have to understand that a seemingly minor change can have a major impact on your career!

The 60,000-Mile Man

Here's another real-life example. Not long ago, I was in Dallas, Texas, doing a program. I was about a quarter of the way into the discussion when a man by the name of Ed stood up and said, "Steve, I'm leaving," and walked out the door. Now, I hadn't had this happen in a very long time. During the break I went up to him and I said, "Ed, why did you walk out?" He said, "Look, Steve, I'm 62 years old. I've been selling for eight years for this company. Every single year I get in my car, drive from Dallas to Oklahoma, down through Arkansas and back to Dallas again. I drive 60,000 miles a year every single year. I don't need you or anybody else to tell me how to sell." I said, "Ed, let me take a wild guess at this. My guess is you're making about the same amount of money every single year." He said, "How did you know?"

I said, "Ed, you're driving 60,000 miles a year and you've been doing it every year for eight years. You have the same amount of appointments every year. You're seeing the same number of people every year. You're doing exactly the same thing every day. If you don't change something, you're not going to change the income." He kind of shrugged and walked away. (I eventually found out *how much* money he was making every year. It wasn't a lot.)

Are you a 60,000-mile salesperson? Are you doing the same things over and over again—and getting the same unsatisfactory result? If so, start thinking about what you're going to change.

Salespeople not only have to know what their ratios are, they must know how to work their ratios. You're going to make sales no matter what you do, but if you don't keep analyzing and keep making adjustments, you're not going to improve over time.

The way I've changed is by growing my company by bringing in new people, by adding more offices, by writing more books. I realized I needed to change something to keep myself sharp. You and I *both* need to change something if we're going to be successful, or else we'll plateau!

Winning the Numbers Game

I talk to many salespeople who actually do know how many people they saw over the past week, but then I say, "What are you going to do differently now?" And they don't know.

If you don't know what you're going to do differently, then you're in trouble. Remember—the best salespeople know how to *work* their numbers.

CHAPTER 3

Where to Look for Leads

What exactly is a prospect? What's the difference between a prospect and a lead?

Many salespeople have difficulty defining the word "prospect." Let's take a careful look at the beginning of the sales process—to see where leads and prospects come from.

Let's say, for example, that I identify a company I want to do business with. Typically, I find it, maybe do a little research on it, and put it in my database. At this point, what do I have? Do I have a prospect? If I really thought about it, I could call it a candidate. I could call it a lead. I could call it a suspect. I could call it any number of things. To me, those are simply opportunities. They're not prospects. There is, however, no question that there is a better chance of making a sale once you've identified a target company than before you've identified it!

Now, suppose I get to the next step—and get an appointment. Two weeks from today I'm going to sit down with a person for the first time to explain my product and try to learn a little bit about what he does and how he does it. Now do I have a prospect?

Well, there is a realistic chance that the person will cancel, postpone, or change that initial date. It won't happen all the time, but it will probably happen often enough for us to factor it in. Therefore, even setting the first appointment does not really mean we're dealing with a prospect. It still is simply an *opportunity,* a *candidate,* or a *lead.*

A prospect is someone who's progressing with you through the steps of the sales process. I'll discuss these steps in more detail in Chapter 10 of this book, but for right now, you should know that those four steps are: the Opening, the Information Stage, the Presentation Stage, and the Closing Stage.

As a practical matter, a prospect is someone who is in steps one, two, or three—someone who is allowing you to open up, get information, and make the proper presentation prior to closing the sale. Another way of thinking about a prospect is that this is somebody who is going to "play ball" with you.

So there are three types of potential customers in the world of sales:

1. A customer, an account, or a client—someone with whom you have closed a sale;
2. A lead, suspect, candidate, opportunity—someone you want to talk with;
3. A prospect—someone you are working with and who's already past the opening step.

Another way to think about it is to use the A=P=S model you've already seen.

Appointments = Prospects = Sales. A prospect, then, is someone who's past the appointment stage, but has not yet formalized the sale.*

---

* As a practical matter, this understanding of "prospect" is most useful in prospect management work. Although this is the literal definition I use in our training, for the purposes of this book, the word "prospect" has also been used to describe someone with whom a salesperson wishes to schedule an appointment. I've adopted this term because it's clearer and less cumbersome than its alternatives. It also reflects common usage among salespeople who make cold calls.

Generating Leads

How do you get to those steps? How do you find your candidates? Let's spend a little bit of time exploring *lead generation.*

There are a number of ways in which we can generate leads. The most important tool you have for lead generation is probably word of mouth—that every single person you know probably knows an average of 250 people. Therefore, it's important that you understand the value of telling people what you do. The problem is that most of us fail to let people know what we do *when we meet them.*

I was at a dinner party the other night; someone came up to me and asked me what I did. I answered him: "Well, I'm the president of D.E.I. Management Group, a sales training firm here in New York City. I'm doing a lot of work with (I named a major company) in the areas of cold calling and prospect management."

My wife thinks I am obnoxious because I'm always using words like these to tell people what I do. I prefer to think of it as being consistent. The reason I'm consistent is that I'm concerned that you—or someone you know—might want to know about my services. Therefore, I want to be consistent in my message to all the people I talk to. If possible, I want to give you a mini-commercial for my business.

When asked what they do, most salespeople reply, "I'm in sales." Of course, that says nothing. You must develop a clear, consistent message that you can use to promote your business.

Everyone who's ever sold anything has thought, at one point or another, about selling to FRAs: friends, relatives, and acquaintances. That is a *big* mistake. It's not productive. It's not effective. It doesn't really work. What's more, it often creates enemies.

Try this instead: use your friends, relatives, and acquaintances *as a way to generate leads.* For example, when was the last time you told your life insurance agent what you do for a living? In order for that life insurance agent to be successful, he or she has to sell to at least 1,200 people. Did you know that? How many of those 1,200 people do you think could use *your* product or services?

Did you know that your accountant probably does about 300 tax returns a year? Does he or she ever call on you for your services? Do you know why? Because you've probably never told your accountant what you do beyond filling in your occupation as "sales" on your tax form. You've probably never told your accountant what *kind* of sales you do. Your accountant almost certainly has clients who could benefit from what you have to offer. Have you ever thought about using your accountant to reach them?

When was the last time you told your physician or your dentist what you do? You never know who's going to be in the dentist's chair or who'll be visiting the doctor's office. Your barber, for that matter, is another source of people you can meet.

Too many salespeople don't take advantage of these opportunities. We *overestimate* how many people know who we are and *underestimate* how many people our acquaintances know. A barber or hairdresser might have as many as 20 customers a day, and yet few salespeople think about using them to generate leads. I give copies of my books to my barber! Every time I write a new book, I give several copies to my physician! (He tells me the books never stay in his office. They are constantly being taken out by salespeople.)

I got a lead at a major computer company through my life insurance agent. He called me shortly after I had sent him a dozen books, and said, "I gave your book to one of my clients, and he happens to work for such-and-such a company. Why don't you give him a call?" Reaching out to such people is a simple but extremely effective way to generate leads.

Civic Organizations

Another way to generate leads is by becoming involved in civic organizations: Rotary, Lions, Kiwanis, Chamber of Commerce, and so on. They're all important. I know most people don't want to bother. But even your church or synagogue gives you a platform to meet people. Why not use every resource available to get more leads?

I've learned over the years that every time I give a speech, one out of 10 people in the audience will come up to me afterward and prequalify themselves. That is, the person will say to me, "You know, you could help my company. You could help me. Here's how. This is what I'm looking for. This is what I want to do." Talk about an effective way to generate leads!

Conferences

On average, you'll get one lead from every 10 people you meet at a conference. A couple of months ago, I went to a conference sponsored by a major entrepreneurial magazine, with 750 business owners in attendance. I walked away with 83 business cards—none of which I actually asked for. People walked up and gave *me* the cards!

The T Call

A *T call* is what happens when you're on an appointment and, after that appointment you go to the right, to the left, and behind you—and come back to the office with three more contacts.

A sales associate once told me that after she got done prospecting at an appointment, she always "did the right thing." What she meant was, whenever she walked out of the appointment, she walked out of the contact's office, turned to the right and saw somebody else. Then she went to the right again and saw somebody else. Of course, I wondered what happened to all the people on the left, but I never asked her. The point is she was using her intuition to gather new contacts, and that helped her build her sales. (Whatever works!)

Newspapers

Newspapers are another good source of leads. You probably already knew that, but consider that most people look at the obvious sections: the business section, and maybe the front page. You should really be looking at the obituaries (not so you can call the person who died, but so you can identify the company he or she worked for), the classifieds, the display ads, and the wedding sections—in addition to the more obvious sections. All of these parts of the papers can give you good information about companies.

I worked with a major computer company about two years ago. We took a copy of the Sunday *Los Angeles Times*, went through the paper, and came up with 198 potential customers that company had never thought about calling before.

Newspapers are an incredible source of leads—especially *old* newspapers. (New ones can actually be trickier, since lots of people call newsmakers the day a story breaks.) Hold on to those newspapers and wait about six to eight weeks; then call, using the techniques you'll learn about later in this book.

Existing Business

Another way to generate leads is through existing business. You have a one in two chance of getting more business from an existing account. You even have a one in four chance of getting business from an inactive account. At the same time, every single business you work with will inevitably suffer from a downturn. They'll change—or their business will change. (Think about IBM. IBM once was famous for its typewriters.

Have you seen a Selectric lately?) Learn to rethink your existing accounts—*while you find new ones.*

The Usual Suspects

And don't forget the standard approaches for new leads: directories, Yellow Pages, White Pages, and lists from list brokers. You should also think about joining clubs where people trade leads and create alliances with other companies.

Some people, because of the nature of their job (e.g., payroll, security, real estate), will know about new companies that are planning to come into your territory. These people can be a tremendous resource for you. Create alliances with them!

Now that you know how to identify the people you'll be calling—what should you say? That's the subject of the next chapter.

CHAPTER 4

Cold Call Mechanics

There are five basic elements to the initial cold call:

1. Get the person's attention
2. Identify yourself and your company
3. Give the reason for your call
4. Make a qualifying/questioning statement
5. Set the appointment

I'm going to cover these in order. As we work our way through this outline, take notes so that you can develop your own cold calling script.

"But I Don't Want to Use a Script!"

Have you recently seen a movie or a television show that you really enjoyed? Sure you have. Did the actors in that drama or that comedy *sound* like they were reading from a script? No. It doesn't sound like a script because the actor has internalized what has to be said. That's what you must do. You have to internalize what you're going to say so it sounds natural.

For example, I've been teaching the *Cold Calling Techniques* program for years. I've learned it, I've memorized it, I've internalized it. I can, therefore, take that program and change it and adjust it as the circumstances require. It always sounds natural.

Do you remember the first time you drove a car by yourself? You were probably so nervous about driving that you actually forgot how to start the car. Or maybe you went through stop signs or you got lost. Now, though, as you drive you don't even think about the various elements of the process.

The objective here is not to "handcuff" you with a script. The objective is to help you develop a script that will help you say what you need to say, while freeing you to pay attention to the prospect's response—which is what's really important.

What is the response? What is the person saying? Are we creating an atmosphere that will make it easy to make positive responses? Or are people responding negatively because we've asked the wrong questions, or asked the right questions in the wrong way? Using a script makes it easier for you to listen for crucial information, since you know exactly what you're going to say.

Here then are the five elements.

1. Get the Person's Attention

I begin a cold call by making a statement that will get attention and open up the conversation.

Let's assume I'm calling you. Depending upon what I say, you're going to respond. No matter what I say, *you're going to respond somehow*. And the better I get at my opening, the more likely I am to get a good response from you!

People Respond in Kind

When you try to get the person's attention, remember that people respond in kind. Salespeople tend to forget this, so they try a nifty opening such as, "If I could save you eight zillion dollars, would you be interested?" How do you feel when someone asks you a question like that?

Gimmicky openings don't work because they produce a gimmicky response. Ask a stupid question, and you'll get a stupid answer. If you ask a reasonable question or make a reasonable statement, on the other hand, you're going to get a reasonable answer. *People respond in kind.*

I got a call recently from a stockbroker. He said, "Mr. Schiffman, are you interested in investing in stocks?" I said, "No," because I wasn't. He hung up. End of call. I responded to the question in kind. Now, had he asked me, "Are you presently with a broker?" I would have said, "Yes," because I was with a broker, even though at that point I wasn't interested in reinvesting. But he would have had a conversation, and perhaps the beginning of a new relationship.

Here's another kind of call I get: "Good morning, Mr. Schiffman, Jack Smith calling from ABC Life Insurance Company. Do you have life insurance?" I say, "Yes." I always say yes because I'm responding in kind to that question. I have no reason to say "No." I say, "Yes." He says, "Well, would you be interested in changing?" I say, "No, I'm not." Awkward silence. End of conversation. The person hangs up. I am simply responding in kind to the questions! Now, had he said to me, "Gee, I'm just curious, why did you buy the life insurance you did? I would have said to him, "Well, I've been with my life insurance agent for the last 17 years. He's a good friend of mine." The salesperson could have used that information to move the sales call along. (Later, I'll show you how to get all the information you need to get to turn a call like this around.) But I never hear that question.

Another call I got recently went like this: "Good morning, Mr. Schiffman, this is XYZ Stock Brokerage House. We'd like to come over to your office and review your 401K plan for your company." I said, "Well, I'm really happy with what we've got." He said, "Okay," and hung up. That happens all the time! Ninety percent of all salespeople make that kind of telephone call. Later on, I'm going to show you how to move beyond that kind of initial obstacle in the conversation. For now, just remember that people really do respond in kind.

I notice that a lot of the stockbrokers who call me try to keep me on the phone by saying, "Well, Mr. Schiffman, if I send you information, would it be okay if I call you back?" You don't need permission to call somebody back. That's foolishness. Just call the person back. If people don't want to take the call, they're not going to take the call. In fact, what most people who sell on the phone don't realize is that the first call is incidental. It doesn't really matter. It's the *second* call that will matter, and it's a waste of time to try to win a promise that the contact will be interested in taking that call.

Don't talk fast or lie or mislead people to get appointments. Some people call and say they've found somebody's wallet, or that a raffle has been won, or they're calling from a doctor's office. Or they say, "Oh, I'm sorry I called this number by mistake." All these gimmicks are terrible. They don't work. They can get you in big trouble. Stay away from them.

I remember doing a program years ago for a company where the salespeople were taught to ask for the wrong name when making the cold call. If they were calling Bill Smith, they would say, "Can I speak to John Smith?"

Inevitably, the secretary or assistant would say, "There's no one here by that name. There's a Bill Smith." They say, "No, I want John Smith."

"There's a Bill Smith."

"Oh, then it must be his brother. Can I speak to him, please?"

So, Bill Smith gets on the phone because he can't figure out who would be calling him with the wrong first name. It doesn't make sense, especially if the name's a little bit odd. So he takes the call and immediately the salesperson says, "Oh, hi John," using the wrong name. Bill says, "No, this is Bill." "Oh, I'm sorry; you know something, I was looking at the wrong name. Anyway, let me tell you why I was calling." And then they get into their little script to see if Bill is interested in whatever they're selling. Such an approach is so irritating (and so ineffective) that you shouldn't even think about using it. Believe me, there are far, far more effective strategies for getting appointments!

The Best Way to Get a Person's Attention

Most salespeople think they have to say something unique or provocative to grab a prospect's attention. Such as, "If I could show you a way in which you could . . . ." Actually, that approach builds mistrust and makes your job harder. The easiest, simplest way of opening up and getting the prospect's attention is by saying his or her name. Call up and say, "Good morning, Mr. Jones."

It's that simple. It's so simple it's almost scary.

Think about it. When you were growing up, your parents called you by your name. You responded to that. If you hear your name yelled out in the middle of a crowded room, you respond. So the first way we get someone's attention is by saying, "Good morning, Mr. Jones."

When you analyze a call, you realize that the key points to focus on are the response and the turnaround. How well can you handle a response? How well can you turn that response around? Given this basic premise, we have to develop an opening that's going to lead to a response we want. And "Good morning, Mr. Jones," or "Good morning, Bob," does that.

The opening of your call is going to lead to a response. You can anticipate that response. You are then going to produce an appropriate turnaround, which should get the appointment. The key to the call is actually not the opening—

although most salespeople spend an inordinate amount of time worrying about what they're going to say in their opening piece. The reality is no matter *what* you say in the opening, people are going to respond to you, and you can prepare for those responses.

Most people will respond positively to a positive-sounding call. Usually, if you speak politely and intelligently to people, they'll speak politely and intelligently to you. There will be a response in kind.

Even a hang up is a response. If you're getting hung up on an awful lot, then the odds are you're probably being too aggressive. Ask yourself: what's turning people off? (Fortunately, if you follow the script we're developing and deliver it confidently and professionally, you won't run into many hang ups.)

2. Identify Yourself and Your Company

If I called you up and simply said, "Good morning, Mr. Jones, this is Steve Schiffman from D.E.I. Management Group," you probably would not know who I was—or what D.E.I. Management Group was—and you probably wouldn't give me the kind of response I wanted. Therefore, I have to go further. I have to build a brief introduction, or *commercial*, into the call. For example, I could say, "Good morning, Mr. Jones, this is Steve Schiffman from D.E.I. here in New York City. We're a major sales training company that's worked with over 450,000 salespeople."

3. Give the Reason for Your Call

Now, the third step, the reason for the call, becomes important. Let's go back to the concept of the man in Times Square who holds his hand out. When he holds his hand out, he does eventually get a response. But when he holds his hand out and adds a cup, and adds a bell, and uses a sign, and walks after people, what he's really doing is increasing the chances that he'll get a *better* response.

When calling for an appointment, I suggest you say the following: "The reason I'm calling you today specifically is to set an appointment."

Now, if that were all I said, if that were my entire program, what do you think would happen? I would get appointments.

Not sure? Well, think about it. If you called a million people, and you said that a million times, would one person give you an appointment? If all you said was "The reason I'm calling you today specifically is to set an appointment," would one person give you an appointment? Absolutely; probably a lot more than one! On the other hand, if you *don't* give the person any idea whatsoever of what you're calling for, what's going to happen? Not much! You have to send a message. You have to let the other person know what you want.

We have a relatively new assistant in our office. She was in Rome, Italy, a number of years ago when she was a student. She was a junior in high school and had been away from home for a while; one day, because she was very hot and tired, she happened to sit down on some church steps. She was wearing a baseball cap, and she took the cap off and put it down in front of her. Lo and behold, people started dropping money in the hat! She was in shock. She couldn't believe it actually happened. Her mother later asked her, "What on earth did you look like, if people started to do that?" But that's not the point. The point is that by putting her hat down, she conveyed that she was interested in receiving money. Even though she didn't mean to send that message, that's the message she sent. She got a response. People dropped lira into her hat. But notice: *she had to put the hat out in order for that to happen.*

If you don't say, "The reason I'm calling is to set an appointment," then no one can say "yes" to the idea of getting together for an appointment. Remember the cup, the bell, and the sign. If I simply say, "The reason I'm calling today is to set an appointment," someone will see me. In fact, my experience is that something like one person out of 12 will see you simply because that person is not sure what you're calling about and will agree to meet with you *because you asked*. Now do you see why it begins to make sense just to ask for an appointment in a straightforward way?

I can enhance that third element of the script. Instead of simply saying, "The reason I'm calling is to set an appointment," I can turn it into something more compelling by saying, for instance, "The reason I'm calling you today specifically is to set an appointment so I can stop by and tell you about our new sales training programs and how they can increase the productivity of your sales force."

Notice that what I've just said *paints a picture* for Mr. Jones. I've really given him a reason for my call. I've talked about increasing productivity. I've actually given him some reasons we should get together. The call is now very directed. I'm not calling to introduce myself. I'm not calling to send a business card. I'm not calling to ask permission to call again. I'm not calling to ask Mr. Jones any questions. And I'm certainly not calling to close the sale! *I'm calling to set an appointment.* That's it.

This point is very important to any salesperson who hopes to be more effective at cold calling. You're calling to set the appointment . . . not to do anything else.

4. Make a Questioning or Qualifying Statement

Now, I'm going to add a questioning statement that's going to allow the prospect an opportunity to respond to me in kind— favorably. The question that I'm going to ask has to be based on my reason for calling Mr. Jones.

My qualifying or questioning statement has to follow easily and logically from that statement. It has to be a reasonable and nonmanipulative extension of what's gone before.

So what am I going to say? I could say, "Mr. Jones, are you interested in having qualified salespeople?" The problem is, that kind of question can produce a negative response. Because there are actually people who will say "no" in response to that question: "No, I'm not interested in increasing my sales." (Anyone who's ever tried to sell using such a question knows this is a fairly common kind of response.)

A better way to start out is, "Mr. Jones, I'm sure that you, like a lot of the other companies that I work with . . . " and here I insert some real names. I might mention a computer company, an HMO, or a life insurance company. It could sound like this: "I'm sure that you, like ABC Company, are interested in having a more effective sales staff." We now have a name inserted as a reference. Mr. Jones is much more likely to say, "Yes, I'm interested."

5. Set the Appointment

Suppose Mr. Jones does say that. Now I'm ready to set the appointment. Here's how:

> *Steve:* That's great, Mr. Jones, then we should get together. How about Tuesday at 3:00?

That's it. Look at it again! You are simply going to say something like the following: "That's great, Mr. Jones, then we should get together. How's Tuesday at 3:00?" Be specific. The request *must* be this direct, this brief, and this specific. Don't change it!

Most salespeople don't want to take this approach. They want to say, "Well, that's great! Then we should get together.

What's better for you—this week or next week?" "What's better for you—Monday or Tuesday?" "What's better for you—morning or afternoon?" "What's better for you—2:00 P.M. or 3:00 P.M.?"

What I've just shown you is very different. I've said, "How about getting together Tuesday at 3:00?" Now the discussion focuses on *when* we're going to get together, not *whether* we're going to get together. Now I have a better chance of getting the appointment.

The biggest mistake most salespeople make is that they fail to ask directly and specifically for the appointment. If you wish to benefit from this program, *you must pose the request for an appointment exactly as I have outlined it here.* When I say, "Let's get together Tuesday at 3:00," I'm being specific, and I'm going to get a response in kind—that is, a specific answer about the appointment on Tuesday at 3:00—because *people respond in kind.*

All Together Now

So here's what one script might sound like:

> *Steve:* Good morning, Mr. Jones, this is Steve Schiffman from D.E.I. here in New York City. We're a major sales training company that's worked with more than 450,000 salespeople. The reason I'm calling you today specifically is so I can stop by and tell you about our new sales training program and how it can increase the productivity of your sales force. I'm sure that you, like ABC, are interested in having a more effective sales staff—(Positive response.) That's great, Mr. Jones. I think we should get together. How's Tuesday at 3:00?

How Not to Set an Appointment

A good friend I'll call Louie makes one of the classic ineffective cold calls. Louie calls and says:

> *Louie:* Good morning, Mr. Jones, this is Louie Blank from the Blank Company here in Boston. The reason I'm calling you today is to see if you might be interested in learning a little bit more about our company.

Inevitably people say:

> *Prospect:* Sure, would you send me a brochure?" or "Sure, send me some literature." Or, "Do you have anything you can mail me?" Or, "Thank you for calling. Send me something."

Louie then gets into a whole conversation about what he'll send you. He never asks for the appointment until it's too late. People are simply responding in kind to his question: "Would you like to learn more about us?"

You must emphasize that you're calling to set an appointment. You can't state any other goal for the call. If you do, you're in trouble. Here is an example of what I mean. I got a call from a stockbroker that went something like this:

> *Stockbroker:* The reason I'm calling you today is to introduce myself and my company.

> *Steve:* Hey, nice to meet you.

> (He didn't know what to say to that. But that's why he's calling me, right?)

> *Stockbroker:* Well, we're XYZ Company.

Steve: That's fine.

Stockbroker: Anyway, would you be interested in getting some material about us?

Steve: Absolutely.

Stockbroker: By the way, I'm just curious, what kind of stocks do you have?

The problem is that, at this point, he's lost momentum. And let's face it, people don't want to reveal the type of stocks they have to a complete stranger! When a salesperson (in this case, a man) calls me up, he should ask for an appointment. That's what he wants. He's calling for my business. That usually means he wants to meet me. Why not say that?

When Do You Call?

One of the most common questions I encounter is, "When should I call?" I call between 7:35 and 8:30 A.M. I have my first appointment scheduled somewhere between 7:45 and 8:30 A.M. By 9:00 A.M. I'm usually done with my cold calls.

You should find the best time for you, but just as important, you should avoid calling when everybody else is calling! I remember doing a training program for a production company in New York City. One discussion went like this:

Steve: What time do you call?

Salesperson: I call at 11:00 A.M.

Steve: Why do you do that?

Salesperson: Well, I get in about 10:00 so that's the best time for me to call—11:00.

Steve: Do you get through?

Salesperson: Well, no, they're always in meetings, but I leave messages.

Steve: Why don't you call at 8:00?

Salesperson: I never thought to do that.

Steve: Why don't you do that?

Salesperson: I'd have to get in early.

Steve: Okay. Get in early.

You have to find the best time for your situation. I've had salespeople call me as late as 10:00 P.M. on a Friday, and I've called people as late as 7:00 P.M. on a Friday. I've even made calls on Saturday. If you haven't thought about that, you might be interested to learn that, in many industries (like mine), Saturday happens to be a pretty good day to call and reach heads of companies.

Getting Past the Gatekeeper

Perhaps you're running into the same problem I once did—getting past the gatekeeper. Consider the following story.

A number of years ago, when this book was first published, I got a call from my editor, who told me that a major company in Chicago had bought 400 copies of my book. He suggested I call them.

I thought to myself, "This is definitely a lead." If that's not a lead, what is a lead? I called the contact at this major Chicago corporation. I got him on the phone and he told me the organization was using my material. They trained with it. He said my program was a fantastic program.

I asked for an appointment: "I've got an idea. Let's you and I get together so we can talk about it. Let me show you how I work. Let me show you some of the things I do."

He told me he was the wrong person to meet with and that there was someone in New York City to talk with who set up training.

I called that person in New York City the next day. The secretary answered the phone. The conversation went like this:

Secretary: What's it about? What are you calling in reference to?

Steve: Well, I was speaking to Mr. John Jones in Chicago and he suggested I give Mr. Peters a call.

Secretary: Well, what is it the nature of the call?

Steve: It's about sales training.

Secretary: I'm sorry, we're not interested.

Steve: Wait a minute. I know you're using 400 copies of my book. I know that your managers are training with my program. Can I speak to your boss?

Secretary: No, we're not interested.

And around and around we went. I'm not insulting secretaries now; I'm just telling you the kind of problem you're likely to run into with gatekeepers.

What do you think I did? What would you do? Salespeople I tell this story to say that they would have called back the person in Chicago, or mailed a letter complaining about the secretary, or even called the president of the company.

The only approach I can recommend is what I actually did. I called at 6:30 P.M. I got through directly to the person I was trying to reach in the first place. And I got the appointment. I realized that I was not going to get through the gatekeeper, but I also realized that there was no real need to "get through" that barrier.

What I did instead was simply call late at night. You might call early in the morning. The point is, there was no reason for me to keep talking to the gatekeeper. In fact, you're going to get through 50 percent of the time no matter what you do, so why get hung up with gatekeepers?

Don't Make Repeat Calls

Not long ago, a participant in a program I did in Chicago said to me, "Every single time I call this company, the receptionist gives me a hard time."

What's wrong with her statement? I'll tell you what's wrong with it. The phrase "every single time" told me right away that she was calling this company too many times!

I asked her how many other people she could call. She responded, "Well, gosh, there's a zillion."

I told her to call those people instead! "Don't call that company. If somebody gives you a hard time, say, 'Thank you very much, have a good day,' and hang up. Then call someone else." Don't take abuse on the phone. You don't need it. There are always other people to call.

A "Bad" Day to Call?

A number of years ago one of our trainers was conducting a program on the Friday afternoon before Labor Day weekend, which is perhaps your biggest nightmare in terms of selling times. After all, who's in the office on the Friday before Labor Day? Who's going to be in to take your call, or, for that matter, anybody else's call?

The program was drawing to a close late in the afternoon. The trainer finished and said, "Thank you very much for coming. Have a wonderful Labor Day." All the representatives got ready to walk out the door, ready to go home. After all, it was 4:00 on the Friday before Labor Day weekend.

The senior vice president stood up and asked where everyone was going.

The representatives replied, "It's Labor Day. We're going to go to the beach."

The VP replied, "Well, look, you have an extra hour. Why don't you get on the phone?"

So now they're facing every salesperson's worst nightmare—it's Friday, 4:00, on Labor Day weekend—and they're supposed to set up appointments. (It's also every sales trainer's worst nightmare—it's not the way most of us would like to test how effective our training is.) The trainer called me up and asked what he should do. I told him to let them make the calls.

An hour later they finished with these numbers: 244, 112, 44. Translation: They dialed 244 people in that hour. They spoke to 112 people and they set up an incredible 44 brand-new appointments!

The program you're learning, the script you're developing right now, *works*. If that story doesn't prove it, nothing does!

Six Specific Telephone Tips for Cold Calling

Here are six specific tips that are going to help you be more effective on the phone. You should be doing these six things in order to implement the program successfully. It's crucial that you do all six, even though each one on its own will help you become more successful in making appointments.

1. Use a Mirror

This is a great $1.79 investment. Go out to a drugstore or specialty store and buy a small hand mirror. Take the mirror and put it where you can see it and look at yourself while you're making calls. You're going to smile while you make calls. Why? When you smile, those "smile" muscles affect your larynx. The result is, you sound better. In fact, you're going to sound better than your competition—the person who's not using the mirror. This gives you an edge.

One of my favorite stories is the one about the sales representative I worked with who sold a tree-pruning service. When I called his customers, they always said, "He made the tree sing." In other words, people could envision the benefits of when he was selling, simply by listening to him. He used his voice very effectively.

Sometimes your voice becomes squeaky because your back neck muscles are pulling on your vocal cords. This makes for a squeaky sound. The smiling relieves this pulling. That's why the mirror is so important—it makes you smile!

2. Use a Timer

Know how much time it takes you to make a good call.

This is important because you don't want your calls to be any longer than they need to be. If it typically takes you two or three minutes to set the appointment, don't go further than those two to three minutes.

Here's another important rule: *Block out your calling time.*

I told you earlier in this book that I make 15 cold calls, speak to seven people, and usually set up one new appointment every day. It takes me approximately 40 minutes each and every day to do that. Accordingly, each and every day I'm not training I schedule 40 minutes for cold calling.

About three years ago I was in Indianapolis doing a program for a major oil company. There was a man in the back of the room who had said nothing for two whole days. I tried to get him to participate. He took notes, he was observant, he listened, but he never once volunteered to participate in the program.

Finally, at the end of the cold calling training, he raised his hand, stood, and asked, "How long does it take you to make those calls?" I said, "Well, it takes me about 40 minutes a day to make my 15 calls." He asked, "How do you do that?" I answered, "I block out the time. In other words, I make an appointment every single day with myself to make those calls."

He said to me, "Steve, the appointment you make with yourself, that 40-minute appointment you make with yourself each and every day, is really what gives you your entire year's worth of business."

This was the most insightful thing that anyone had said to me in years. The 40-minute prospecting appointment that I make and keep with myself does in fact guarantee me my income. His observation had been worth the wait!

3. Practice!

Once you finish this book, it's going to take you a minimum of three hours of practicing the principles you learn here for you to be successful.

When I first started my business I was *not* a good cold caller. I simply could not get appointments. (In fact, the reason I learned how to make appointments was that I *needed* to make the appointments.) Once I realized that there were certain things that I had to say and that I had to learn how to say them, I practiced. My wife Anne and I sat at the kitchen table going back and forth with role plays until I learned the responses and developed the right phone approach. It was the best time investment I ever made.

So do what I did. Practice. It will take you three hours or so, but if you practice properly, those three hours will be the most productive hours of your entire sales career.

When I say this to salespeople, they often say, "Well, I don't need to practice. I make cold calls every day." That's not really practicing. Practicing means drilling. Get someone to help you: your spouse, your friend, whoever. Make that person work with you until you get your cold calling responses down perfectly.

It just doesn't make sense to practice on a prospect! You're thinking about too many things; your mind is focused on connecting with that person, not on learning the fundamentals.

4. Keep a Record of Your Calls

In other words, learn to manage your numbers. Successful salespeople don't merely *know* their numbers; they know how to use their numbers, how to analyze the ratios and set appropriate goals based on them. Get in the habit of tracking three things: the number of dials, the number of completed calls, and the number of appointments you get.

A number of years ago a salesperson told me that it took him 400 dials to set up an appointment. I asked him, "Well, how many people did you actually connect with?" He didn't know that number. Therefore, there's really no way to determine whether his number was good or bad. Okay, it wasn't great. But consider this: for all we know, he could have spoken to 400 people to get only one appointment—which is, admittedly, terrible. On the other hand, suppose he only *spoke* to two out of the 400 people he dialed—and still got one appointment. Then, from a certain point of view, he's doing great! The question then becomes—what's keeping him from getting through 398 of 400 times?

What are your numbers? How do they fit into your revenue goals? What do you expect the numbers to be? What's your desired end result?

Usually when I'm doing a program I ask salespeople how many cold calls they've made in a year. They often don't know their numbers. Worse than that, they don't know the number of sales they *need to complete* at the end of the year. Therefore, even if they knew their numbers, they wouldn't have known whether or not that number was sufficient to deliver on the goal!

Determine for yourself what numbers you need. Find out how many appointments you must make each and every day in order to make the total number of sales you need at the end of the year.

5. Tape-Record Your Calls

In many places it's legal for you to tape-record your calls and then listen to them if you do so for your own use. (You should, however, check whether your state's laws require you to notify the person you're talking to.) I recommend that, for a solid week, you listen to 100 percent of your calls. Pay attention to both sides of the conversations. How does what you say sound? What responses do you get? Listen to 75 percent of your calls the second week, 50 percent the third week, and 10 percent thereafter, and I guarantee you will get a one-third increase in first appointments.

I have received many letters over the years from people who've told me how much listening to their own calls has helped them improve their results. The reason this works is obvious—you get to listen to the mistakes you're making. Once you hear and truly acknowledge a mistake, you're probably never going to make that mistake again.

6. Stand Up

Stand up when you make your calls! For many years, I worked at a stand-up desk. My chair was a stool, the telephone was raised. I was one-third more productive than I had been when I was sitting down.

Most of us sit down and start to make our cold calls at the end of the day. There we are dialing away, tired, exhausted, bent over our desks and (let's face it) not sounding very good.

When you stand up and make cold calls, you're going to sound more animated (especially if you make your calls while you still have some energy). You're going to feel better about yourself. You're going to sound better, and, once again, it's going to give you the edge that you need to be more successful.

Implement!

All of these techniques are tried and true. They've been proven to be effective time after time. But these ideas, like all of the things you're learning about in this book, will not help you if you don't implement them. (And by the way, the same ideas will help those whose job it is to *close* sales on the phone, rather than set appointments.*)

Having said all this, let me be very clear on one point. I think it's a fallacy for people who write sales books to claim their system (or any system) is going to work all the time. My approach isn't going to work on every call, but I can promise you this: If you follow this program, it will get you one out of 10 more appointments.

If this program will increase your appointments by *10* percent, is it worth trying? Of course it is. Look at it this way: If you simply speak to *one* more person on the phone a day, it's worth it. That's over 200 more contacts a year. If you get just one more appointment every single week, that's 50 more appointments than you've got right now. And if you implement the program as it's laid out in this book, that's what you can do.

---

* Hundreds of thousands of people make sales calls on the phone. If this is your assignment, read my book *Stephan Schiffman's Telesales*, also published by Adams Media Corporation. You'll see that it describes how to get business on the phone— by raising key issues early in the game.

CHAPTER 5

Turning Around Common Responses

Of course, not everyone says "yes" when you ask for an appointment. It's important to remember, though, that when someone says, "No, I don't want to see you," it's because that person is responding to you in kind. He or she is responding to the question you posed. Don't think of this as an "objection." Think of it as what it is—a response to what you've just said.

The Four Most Common Responses

You're soon going to realize that virtually every initial "no" response falls into one of these four categories:

1. "No thanks, I'm happy with what I have."
2. "I'm not interested."
3. "I'm too busy."
4. "Send me some literature."

The trick is to learn how to anticipate and handle these responses properly.

"No Thanks, I'm Happy with What I Have"

Earlier I told you that our number one competitor is the status quo. For the most part, people really are happy with what they already have. The vast majority of the people you'll speak to will be happy, relatively "set." Otherwise, *they* would have called *you*. And guess what? They're not calling you!

You don't operate a business that's like a pizza parlor. People don't walk in and talk to you because they want to order something from you. You're reversing the process. You're out on the street, as it were, dragging people in for pizza!

And initially, yes, that person says he or she is happy with what's happening now. In fact, at the moment you call that person, he or she is *already* doing something. In other words, you're interrupting that person when you call.

When a Prospect Gives You Lemons, Make Lemonade

I deal with a lot of banks. In fact, my company works with just about every major financial institution in the United States today. A number of years ago I called a bank at 7:00 A.M. and talked to a senior manager—the type who probably shows up at *4:00* A.M. The conversation went like this:

> *Steve:* Mr. Jones, this is Steve Schiffman from D.E.I. Management Group. We're a major sales training company here in New York City, and we've worked with . . .

> *Mr. Jones:* Steve, let me stop you right there.

(It's almost as if he held up his hand.)

> *Mr. Jones:* Let me stop you right there. Steve, we're already doing sales training. In fact, today's the first day of the program.

At this point, he held up the telephone so I could hear the noise of the people getting ready for the meeting. There I am at 7:00 A.M., listening to the sound of someone else starting a sales training session. Noise. How do you think I felt?

Mr. Jones: Can you hear? Phil's coming in right now!

I didn't know who Phil was. (I didn't even care who Phil was.) I listened to the noise, as I'd been instructed. Suddenly, it dawned on me. I shouldn't feel bad. I should feel great! This person has just told me he's a potential customer—he does sales training. So without missing a beat, I said:

> *Steve:* You know something, Mr. Jones, that's great that you're using sales training. A lot of the other banks (and I named several banks that we had worked with) have said the same thing before they had a chance to see how our program, especially the cold calling program, would complement what they were doing in-house. You know something, we should get together. How about next Tuesday at 3:00?

(By the way, every word I'd said to Mr. Jones was absolutely true.)

Mr. Jones: (After a pause.) Okay.

I got the appointment.

Think for a moment about how I did that. What I said was, in essence, "Other people told me exactly the same thing you did. They had the same reaction you did *before* they had a chance to see how what we do complements (fits into, matches, supports) what they're already doing. We should get together. How about next Tuesday at 3:00?"

In other words, I reinforced what Mr. Jones was already doing. I simply said that we could complement what he does, that we fit into that plan, that we could match that plan. I told him that he should look at our programs *because* of what he's already doing. I didn't tell him how to feel about the situation, or pretend I knew how he felt. I simply told him how I felt ("That's great!") and then told him the facts.

Don't say, "I sure can understand that," which is the way most people have been taught to turn around responses. It sounds stupid. It's completely unbelievable. What is there for you to understand at this point in the conversation? Remember: If you speak intelligently with a prospect, the prospect will speak intelligently back to you. People respond in kind. So don't say things like "I know how you feel" or "I can understand that" at this early point in the relationship.

Much of the training salespeople get in cold calling encourages empathy. The problem is, you don't have the vaguest idea how the prospect feels—and it's condescending to say you do. Let's say you're talking to a guy who's 55 years old, and you're just starting in sales. Can you honestly call him and tell him you understand how he feels? No!

Once you understand that your objective is to get in the door, not to empathize, you'll start to see how the sales process really works.

Tell the Truth!

Think again about what I did in the call I just told you about. The bank manager was happy with his current service and I *still* managed to get in the door. Why? Because instead of playing word games, I told him the truth: I'd heard similar reactions from other companies in his industry before they saw how what we offered complemented what they were already doing.

If that's true for you, too (and I'm betting it is), then you have a strategy for dealing with the "I'm happy" response.

"I'm Not Interested"

Let's take a look at the next most common response. Let's say I call someone up and he says to me, "Steve, look, we're really not interested." Has that ever happened to you? Sure. Now here's the big question: Have you ever *sold* to someone who initially wasn't interested? Your answer has to be yes, because that's what sales is. *Sales is selling to somebody who wasn't interested prior to your call.* Again, if they were "interested," they would have called you.

So here's what I say:

> *Steve:* Well, Mr. Jones, a lot of people had the same reaction you did when I first called—before they had a chance to see how what we do will benefit them.

Isn't that the truth? Well, then say that. While you're at it, why not tell the person the names of the relevant companies you've worked with? If you have appropriate referrals, you should certainly use them, and this is the perfect time. Tell your contact that the XYZ Company, the ABC Company, and the National Widget Company all had the *same* reaction he did *before* they had a chance to see how what you do could benefit them. It's the truth.

"I'm Too Busy"

The third most frequent response is "I'm too busy." In other words, you call somebody and they say, "Steve, I'm too busy. I can't talk now." Typically, salespeople react to that by asking, "Well, what's a better time to call?"

In my seminars, I have plenty of discussions like this:

Salesperson: Steve, I have to leave the program to make a call, because Mr. Jones said to call him at 11:00.

Steve: Really? Tell you what, we'll take a break and we'll just sit here and wait for you.

Salesperson: Oh, no, I'll be on the phone.

Steve: Trust me. We'll take a break, you'll be back in a minute or two.

Of course, that's exactly what happens. Think about it. Nine times out of ten, Mr. Jones has no reason to sit there and wait until the stroke of 11:00 for a salesperson to call him.

For Mr. Jones, specifying 11:00 was a way to get rid of you. That's all it was.

But how do you deal with the prospect who says, "I'm too busy?" There is an effective strategy you can use.

Let's say I call Mr. Jones, and he says that he's too busy to talk. Instead of asking, "What's a better time to call?" I say: "Mr. Jones, the only reason I was calling was to set an appointment. Would next Tuesday at 3:00 be okay?"

Look at what I just did. I took that first response, "Look, I'm too busy to talk," and responded with, "Oh—well the only reason I was calling was to set up an appointment." After all, you don't really want to have a conversation now! You want to get the appointment. The truth is, the other person doesn't want to have a conversation now, either.

Now the prospect generally will not agree to this suggestion. Instead, the prospect will probably raise another of the standard responses we're discussing. For example:

Mr. Jones: Well, I'll tell you the truth. I'm really happy with what I've got.

Now I can go back to the response I've prepared for that kind of statement:

> *Steve:* Oh, that's great! A lot of people tell me the same thing before they have a chance to see what we do complements what they're doing.

Understand: The person hasn't yet said he won't see you. Now you've got another response, and you can deal with that.

Note: Don't try to turn around more than three answers at this point. Instead, you can simply say: "Okay, I'll call you back later." (And mean it!)

"Send Me Some Literature"

This next response is probably the most difficult to handle. This is the person who says to you, "Look, do me a favor. Mail me something." That response is difficult because the premise behind mailing something is that the prospect will look at it, will think about it, will respond to it intelligently, and then when you call, you'll have an intelligent conversation about it. That's a real problem! Too often, salespeople translate "send literature" this way:

> "Well, Mr. Salesperson, I might be interested in what you have to sell. Why don't you send me something. Let me look at it, really study it; then call me. We'll have an intelligent conversation and I, who by that point will have read it all, will let you tell me more about what you offer."

The problem is that 90 percent of all salespeople we surveyed said that their mail somehow never gets through to the person they mailed it to. Obviously that's not correct. Think about it. Your credit card bills, your telephone bill, and your bank statement all get to you. And yet sales material never gets through?

It got through. Your prospects just don't remember it. They don't care about it. They didn't read it. The secretary threw it out. It doesn't really matter what happened to your material, does it? The point is that this approach *doesn't move the sales process forward*. It doesn't get you closer to an appointment.

Here's how to turn that response around. When the prospect says to you, "Look, why don't you mail me something?" Just say, "Can't we just get together? How about next Tuesday at 3:00?"

It's as simple as that! "Can't we just get together? How about next Tuesday at 3:00?" Don't get any fancier than that. If you don't get the appointment, nine times out of 10, the person will say, "Well, I'll tell you the truth. I'm pretty happy with what we're doing." And you know how to respond to that!

Don't Forget to Listen!

Listen to what the other person says. Suppose you hear: "Look, I'm really happy with what I'm doing because I'm using the ABC Widget Company to come in here and work on this."

Now you can say, "We really *should* get together because of what you're doing. My experience is that we can definitely complement ABC."

The First Response Isn't Worth Fighting Over

Typically, when you listen carefully, you'll find that the first response isn't really the obstacle it sounds like.

A number of years ago, I called a major bank. This is how the conversation went when I asked a decision-maker at the bank for an appointment.

The person said, "Well, I'll tell you the truth. We're really happy with what we've got and everything's okay."

I responded to that by suggesting that what we did could complement what he was already doing.

He said, "Oh, well, the real problem is that we have no budget."

I said, "Well, that's okay, let's get together anyway."

And we got together!

This was the first major sale that I ever made—$75,000. I was so excited on the drive home that I got a speeding ticket! I learned a very important lesson from that call. What I learned was that the first response had very little validity. *Once I handled the first response properly, the second response emerged.*

In other words, responses roll into each other. They're not isolated. Very rarely does anybody simply say "no." People usually say "no," and add a story of some kind: "No, I'm not interested because this is what we're doing now."

My experience is that it's the *second* response that really matters. Once you understand that, you can start to see how well what you're suggesting is going to work. The key is the second response, not the first.

Once you understand this premise, you'll be much more effective in getting appointments. The approach I'm suggesting can be applied to a whole range of potential responses.

My company has a salesperson in London who gets so many appointments it would make your head spin. No matter what a prospect says to her on the phone, she says: "Oh, well, that's okay. Why don't we get together anyway?" Of course, that strategy only makes sense if you use it intelligently and judiciously. Consider the following:

Prospect: Well, you know, really we're not interested.

You: Oh, that's okay. Why don't we get together anyway?

Prospect: Well, we just signed a contract with a major competitor.

You: Well, that's okay. Why don't we get together anyway?

Prospect: Uh, well, we hate your company.

You: Well, that's okay. Why don't we get together anyway?

Prospect: Because I hate *you.*

The point is, though, that fighting with a prospect over the first response (or any response, for that matter) is foolish. Often, I ask salespeople, "What do you say when the person on the phone says he's happy with what he has now?" You know how they respond? "Well, Mr. Prospect, I sure could make you happier!" That's a challenge, and a pointless one.

If the potential client says, "No, we're not interested," many salespeople offer a different equally pointless challenge: "Well, I don't know what exactly it is that you're not interested in; I haven't told you what I'm calling about yet." Not the best strategy. If a potential client says, "I'm too busy to talk," many salespeople, as we've seen, will say, "Well, what's a good time to call you back?" That approach isn't going to work, either. And when people say, "Send literature," some salespeople respond, "It will only take five minutes. Please, sir, let me come in. I'll get on my hands and knees and I'll do a very quick pre-sentation. If you don't like it, I'll be out in five minutes." I've had salespeople tell me they actually put a watch down in front of the person. "Here's my five minutes," they say, "You let me know when it's up." What foolishness.

You and I are professionals. We should be treated as such. What's more, we need to behave like professionals if we expect to be treated like professionals. The person who's subservient or submissive to the prospective client is not going to be perceived as professional.

Many years ago, I said to a prospective client, "This will only take me five minutes." I'll never forget what happened next. That person said, "Okay, you have five minutes." I went in to the appointment and I started speaking. After five minutes, he stood up and walked out. Foolishness. I created that for myself. But I never will again.

You're a professional. Never forget that as you deal with the responses you hear on the phone.

CHAPTER 6

The Ledge

The concept of the Ledge in a cold call is unique to my company. As the name suggests, the Ledge is something you can step on—something you can use to regain your footing. A Ledge allows you to handle an extended conversation during your call. It doesn't limit your conversation. You use the Ledge to support your conversation as you're uncovering what it is that they do, how they do it, when they do it, where they do it, who they do it with, and why they do it that way. Then the Ledge lets you take that information and you turn it around to say, "You know something? That's why we *should* get together."

Welcome to the Ledge

A Ledge *uses the first question or negative response as a foothold to turn an extended phone-prospecting conversation around*.

Probably every salesperson in the United States has had an occasion to over-talk, to get so involved in a conversation that he or she forgets the reason for the call. Remember: The number one reason you're calling is to *set the appointment*. But it's easy to get involved in everything *but* an appointment discussion. Let me give you an example of how that happens.

When I make a cold call, I sometimes hear the prospect say, "Really? I might be interested in that. Tell me about it now."

These are truly terrible words, because you don't know enough to make any meaningful recommendation, and you can't simply refuse the prospect's request. You can't say, "No, it's a secret. I won't tell you about what we do." (I guess you could, but it probably wouldn't help you move the sales process forward.) So you can't really say no. And yet your aim is not to sell, but to set an appointment. So you have to prepare.

Ask yourself: What are you going to say when somebody you've never sat down with says to you, "Tell me about it right now. Tell me everything about your widgets. Go."

What are you going to do? Well, first and foremost, you're going to answer the prospect. That's your instinct, and that's fine. But that can't be *all* you do. Why? Consider the following exchange.

Prospect: How long has your company been in business?

You: We've been in business for the last 17 years.

Prospect: No kidding! Well, tell me how you did that.

(So you elaborate on that. You pass along a couple of success stories. Then your contact says:)

Prospect: That's a very impressive story. Tell me how you did that.

(Now you elaborate. You offer all the specifics about that success story. And all of a sudden the person says:)

Prospect: Oh, well, that may have worked then, but we don't really need that.

And the conversation is over, because the person you're talking to is right. You started talking before you knew anything of consequence about the other person. The result? What you've just described doesn't match up with this prospect.

How do you avoid this outcome?

Here's an example of a prospecting call I made recently that will prepare you to use and understand the Ledge.

> *Steve:* Good morning, Mr. Jones, this is Steve Schiffman from D.E.I. Management Group. We're a major sales training firm here in New York City . . .

> *Mr. Jones:* No kidding! You know, we're thinking about doing training. So tell me—what do you guys do?

> (Again—I can't say to him, "I can't tell you what we do.")

> *Steve:* Well, we've been in business for 17 years. We've trained over 450,000 salespeople. I've written 12 books.

> *Mr. Jones:* What kind of programs do you do?

> *Steve:* Well, I do cold calling, prospect management, and . . .

> *Mr. Jones:* Really! How do you train cold calling?

I give a brief answer. The call is going well. Then, somewhere in the conversation he says to me, "Well, what's your price?" And I have to deal with that.

We've had a friendly conversation, so I can't say, "Our pricing is classified." Instead, I say, "The range is between X and Y." I answer the question. And Mr. Jones responds by saying, "Wait a second, that's way too expensive."

Instead of defending myself, instead of fighting him on that, I simply say, "Mr. Jones, a lot of our customers initially had the same reaction until they actually got a chance to see the benefits. You know, we really *should* get together."

In other words, I use his response, his negative response in this case, as a reason we should get together. Look at it again:

Mr. Jones: Gee, I'm not sure that fits what we're doing here.

Steve: You know, that's what other people said who decided to work with us. We really *should* get together. How's Tuesday at 2:00?

Or:

Mr. Jones: Gee, I'm not sure that's right for us.

Steve: Some other people we work with now had the same reaction at first. That's why we *should* get together. How's Tuesday at 2:00?

No matter what he says, *that*'s why Mr. Jones and I should get together. Once you understand that principle and implement it, your appointment total will improve.

Using the Ledge to Get an Appointment

The salespeople we train use the Ledge to regain control of a conversation by asking a question. This is an extremely effective tool; take a look at how it works.

I called a potential customer recently; the person told me that his organization didn't use sales training.

Prospect: Steve, we're not interested in sales training. We don't believe in it here.

Steve: I'm just curious . . . if you don't use sales training, what is it that you do? What do you do with your new salespeople? Just how do you work with them?

Prospect: Well, we don't really train them. We simply have them work with the managers and when they're ready, they go out on their own.

Steve: That's great, Mr. Jones! Then we should get together, because we work with a lot of other companies that have done the exact same thing. How about next Tuesday at 3:00?

And I got the appointment. That "I'm just curious" question allowed me to gain a foothold, to resume control of the conversation. That's the Ledge in action.

I used the information he gave me about what he does as a reason to get together. People who are successful at scheduling appointments understand the power of this simple concept.

Here's another example of how to use the Ledge:

Prospect: Headquarters makes that kind of decision.

Steve: Okay. I'm just curious, what do you do? What's your role there?

When he answers, I respond, "That's interesting. Based on what you've told me, I think we *should* get together."

Recently, I called up the New York City office of a major company located in Ohio. The person who answered the phone happened to be the branch manager. The conversation went like this:

Branch manager: Steve, I'd love to meet with you but we don't make any decisions here. All the decisions are made in Ohio.

Steve: Oh, well, I'm just curious. What kind of training do you do?

He responded to this by telling me about three different types of training he does. Then I said, "You know something, we *should* get together, because we really complement those programs."

We ended up scheduling a meeting. When we got together, he said to me, "Steve, I can't make these decisions myself, but I can *get* them made." That meeting turned into a half-million-dollar sale, and it was generated by my use of the Ledge.

Here's another example. When I called the prospect, the conversation went something like this:

> *Prospect:* Steve, we're really not working with any other outside trainers. We just signed a contract with someone.
>
> *Steve:* Oh, that's interesting. I'm just curious, who'd you sign with?
>
> *Prospect:* Well, we signed with XYZ Company.
>
> *Steve:* You know what? We *should* get together, because we complement their program.

As you get more experience, you'll start to learn more sophisticated approaches. For example, I called another company and got an appointment like this:

> *Prospect:* Look, we just signed a contract with another training company.
>
> *Steve:* Well, are you using the Brand X Selling Solution?
>
> *Prospect:* No, we're not using Brand X. We're using Brand Y.
>
> *Steve:* Oh, then we really *should* get together, because what we do complements Brand Y.

I can throw out any company, any kind of training program. He will respond to me in kind by correcting me and telling me who his company uses. (Prospects love to correct salespeople.) I always say, "Then we *should* really get together."

You've got the basic principle now. No matter what the person says to you, you're going to say, "We really *should* get together."

Talking to the Wrong Person

Another mistake salespeople make involves the way they respond when somebody says, "I'm the wrong person to talk to." Most salespeople then ask, "Who's the right person?" Never ask that. Instead, when the other person says, "I'm the wrong person," you should say, "Gee, I'm just curious. What is it you do?" And no matter what they say to that, unless you're *absolutely* sure this is the wrong person, you're going to say, "Oh, then you know what? We *should* get together."

If they're really not the right person, they're going to let you know. They might say, "I'm in charge of bricklaying here at the foundry." If you're selling video postproduction, then that's really not the right person. *Then* you should ask, "Oh, then who *should* I talk to?" And then you can take that name and use it as part of a referral call, which I'll explain later.

A Real Conversation

Once you start using the Ledge, you'll soon realize that you're really having a conversation with your prospect. At this point it's not a sales call, it's a conversation. Initially, my conversation happens to revolve around my desire to get an appointment, while the prospect's conversation is about what they're doing, how happy they are doing it, and why they see no need to change. Often, the Ledge is where the two conversations become one.

So first, most people would be "happy" if I never called in the first place. Think about that. If I didn't call Tuesday, but called Wednesday, would it matter to these people? They're still doing business. The world is still spinning. They don't "need" that call.

If you understand these basic ideas, and use the information you get from your conversations with prospects to create a Ledge in your cold call, I promise you that you will become more effective.

More Examples of the Ledge in Action

A while back, a sales representative who was in one of my programs said, "Steve, we have a problem. This cold calling stuff won't really work for me. You're good at it, but that's because you train it for a living." What he meant, I believe, was that the program is second nature for me, and that, for people who are unfamiliar with it, it *isn't* second nature. And he was right.

At this point in my career (I've been doing this for 27 years), cold calling *is* relatively simple to me. It does come very naturally. For you it may be more difficult. The reason I told you the golf story at the beginning of the book was to make the points that certain aspects of cold calling are not going to be comfortable, and that, initially, you're not always going to like some of the parts of the process.

Whether you're comfortable with the program at first or not, you *can* honestly say, "I can improve my odds. I can get one more appointment a day if I simply employ these techniques." And if you give it an honest try, you're going to do that. When you hear resistance on the phone, you're going to ask a question, and then you're going to say, "That's great. You know something, we *should* get together." That's how the Ledge works.

Let's look at some more examples of the Ledge in action.

Example 1

Prospect: I'm really not interested.

You: A lot of the people we work with said the same thing before they had a chance to see the way in which we complement what they're presently doing.

Prospect: Yeah, but you know, we've had a difficult time with your company before.

You: Can I just ask you a question? Who presently supplies your light bulbs?

Prospect: Well, we use the XYZ Company. We went to them instead.

You: Oh, no kidding. Then we really *should* get together.

Prospect: No, I really don't think so. Why don't you send me information. I'll take a look at it.

You: Can we just get together? How about next Friday at 3:00?

Prospect: No, I'll tell you the truth. I'm really not interested.

You: Okay. Thank you.

(Hang up! You gave it your best shot. Call someone else.)

Example 2

Prospect: You know, we really don't have any kind of budget for that.

You: No kidding. Well, just out of curiosity, are you working with anybody right now?

Prospect: Sure we are. We have the 123 Manufacturing Company right here.

You: Are you using their ABC product?

Prospect: No, we're actually using their BC2 product.

You: Really? Then we *should* get together. How about next Friday at 5:00?

Example 3

Prospect: Why don't you tell me something about your product?

(Note: Remember that you *must* give a brief, direct answer to a prospect's question.)

You: Well, you know something, Mr. Jones, we've been in business for the last 42 years and we've developed a number of ways in which we can substantially reduce wear and tear in the manufacturing process. I'm just curious though, what does your company do?

(Instead of rambling on, you pose a question of your own.)

Prospect: Well, we manufacture customized widgets. We use the ABC product line here.

You: Really? Has that been working for you?

Prospect: Sure it has.

You: Oh, that's great then. We really *should* get together so I can show you the ways we can complement ABC.

Example 4

Prospect: You know, why don't you put something in the mail. Let me take a look at it and I'll give you a call back. I'm really kind of busy right now.

You: Actually, the only reason I called is to set up an appointment. Would next Tuesday be okay?

Prospect: Well, not really. You know, I'll tell you the truth. This is my busiest time of the year.

You: I have an idea. What are you doing four weeks from today?

Prospect: Let me check—nothing.

You: Well, why don't we get together Friday the 11th at 2:00?

Prospect: Okay.

You've now succeeded in scheduling the appointment. Confirm the address and politely *conclude the conversation!* Don't try to sell, and don't get involved in a long, drawn-out discussion.

Be Prepared!

Remember, in each case you're creating a Ledge. You're finding a foothold you can use to turn the conversation around.

Sometimes, though, you won't even need the Ledge:

> *Steve:* Good morning, Mr. Jones, this is Steve Schiffman from Widget Management here in New York. I don't know if you know who we are, but we're the major supplier of widgets in the area. We've worked with ABC Corporation and 123 Company. Anyway, the reason I'm calling you today specifically is to set up an appointment so I can tell you the way in which we've been successful with other companies. How's Tuesday at 2:00?

> *Mr. Jones:* You know, that sounds great. Come on over.

There *are* calls that sound like that. Be ready for them!

| CHAPTER 7 |

Mastering Third-Party and Referral Calls

Third-party and referral calls are variations on the standard script. Study them. You'll need them!

The Third-Party Call

First, let's look at the third-party endorsement approach to cold calling. It's very easy, and it may even complement the way you're now selling. This is the variation I use, and most of the salespeople we train say this is a very easy model to adapt. I think you're going to enjoy it.

The Basic Steps

The first thing to remember about this approach is that it uses the same basic steps we've already discussed:

- Get the person's attention.
- Identify yourself and your company.
- Give the reason for your call.
- Ask for the appointment.

These are key points that will increase the effectiveness of your calls—no matter what kind of call you're making. Let's examine how they apply to the third-party call.

Get the Person's Attention

I've already told you that the way you get the person's attention is not by saying something gimmicky (like, "Are you interested in making a million dollars?") but by saying the person's name. You can decide on your own approach here. Do you like to say, "Hi, Bob," "Hi, Joe," or "Hi, Jill"? Do you like to say, "Good morning, Mr. Jones"? Whatever you're most comfortable with, that's what you can use. I happen to like to say, "Good morning, Mr. Jones," or "Good afternoon, Mr. Jones." That's going to be my attention statement. I don't need anything more than that.

Identify Yourself and Your Company

I've already indicated that if I said to you, "This is Steve Schiffman from D.E.I. Management Group," the odds are you would not know who that is. So that statement, on its own, is not going to be entirely appropriate in getting an appointment or letting you understand who I am. I need to give you a chance to understand exactly what I'm talking about.

Why? Because when we telephone somebody, that person is not prepared for the call. We're the last thing on that person's mind.

What we're doing, by its nature, requires you to get people to think about something that they weren't thinking about before we called them. In other words, the call doesn't follow the natural course of the person's day. Your prospects are doing what they're doing, and you telephone them and say, "Stop, I need you to do something else." Well, why should they?

We have to give them an opportunity to understand what we're talking about, and then paint a picture for them so they can visualize the process. Here's how to do that.

So far I have "Good morning, Mr. Jones"; that's my opening. Here's my second step:

> "This is Steve Schiffman, I'm the president of D.E.I. Management Group. I don't know if you've ever heard of us, but we're an international sales training company here in New York City. I also have offices in Chicago and Los Angeles. I do a lot of work with . . ."

And now I mention the XYZ, the ABC and the 123 companies in the context of cold calling and prospect management. This is painting the picture. I said key words. I've said *sales training, cold calling, prospect management.* I've mentioned the XYZ, the ABC, and the 123 companies, which are major players, not necessarily in Mr. Jones's area, but still major players in the United States. They're going to be familiar to him.

So I've painted a picture for my prospect. I've allowed him to imagine what it is that this call is about. My prospect can think, "Oh, this is in reference to sales training." Why should I make him wonder, "Huh? What? What's this about?" With this approach, I don't need a gimmicky opening.

Now you focus on a specific success story. You can choose your own references to call just about anyone you want to talk to.

A number of years ago I was working with a major bank. I had trained about 500 of their sales managers to be more effective on the phone. (I got the account because I gave a free speech at a Chamber of Commerce meeting, and a woman came up to me afterward and said she thought I could help the bank she worked for. It happened to be the number three bank in the United States at that time.)

About six or seven weeks after completing the program, I decided that I'd call another bank. It occurred to me that, since one bank was doing something about sales, another bank would probably be trying to do the same thing. If I could help one bank do that better, I could help another. It really had nothing to do with the fact that the organizations were competitors. Once this approach crystallized in my mind, I realized *I had a means of entry into virtually any bank or financial services organization I wanted to call.*

The next day I took a directory, found the name of a senior vice president of another bank, called him up, and said:

"Hello, Mr. Smith. This is Steve Schiffman. I'm the president of D.E.I. Management Group, an international training company here in New York City with offices in New York, Los Angeles, and Chicago. I've done a lot of work with ABC Bank in the areas of cold calling and prospect management." He listened—and he agreed to meet with me!

Take a look now at the third and fourth steps.

Give Reason for Your Call and *Ask for the Appointment*
Continue by saying, "The reason that I'm calling you today specifically* is that I just completed a very successful sales training with the ABC Bank here in New York City. In fact, it increased their appointments by one-third. I'd like to stop by next Tuesday at three and just *tell you about the success I had with the ABC Bank.*"

The beauty of this call is you never say, "What we did for ABC Bank will work for you. You're simply saying that you've worked with another company in this person's industry, and

---

* In seminars, I tell salespeople that they can and should adapt the wording of their scripts to their own situation, but that they should leave certain elements intact verbatim. "The reason I'm calling you today specifically" is one of those elements. Don't alter it; it works just as written. Similarly, you should ask directly for the appointment by specifying a date and time: "How's Tuesday at 2:00?"

you were successful with that company. That's the heart of the third-party endorsement approach.

This approach can work very well across industry lines, too. Look at it again:

> "Good morning, Mr. Blank, this is Steve Schiffman from D.E.I. Management Group, an international training company here in New York City. We're also in Chicago and Los Angeles. We've worked with the XYZ, ABC, and 123 companies in the areas of cold calling and prospect management. The reason that I'm calling you today specifically is I just completed working with U.S. Delivery, a major courier in the Louisville area. I was very successful in showing them ways in which they could increase their sales by actually getting more appointments, which they did. They got thirty percent more appointments. Anyway, what I'd like to do is stop by and tell you about the success I had with U.S. Delivery. How's Tuesday at 3:00?"

The key to this call, once again, is that I'm not telling prospects I can do the same for them. I'm mentioning my success with other companies and asking for an appointment. I'm not making empty promises.

Here's another way I can make this call:

> "Good morning, Mr. Jones, this is Steve Schiffman from D.E.I. Management Group. I'm doing a lot of work with the XYZ, ABC, and 123 companies in the area of cold calling. The reason I'm calling you today specifically is that I just completed working with the Blankety Lumber Company here in the area. I was very successful in showing them ways in which they could increase their lumber sales by getting more appointments. What I'd like to do is stop by next Tuesday at 3:00 and just tell you about the success that I had with the Blankety Lumber Company."

I can also make this approach generic. I can say:

> "Good morning, Mr. Jones, Steve Schiffman, from D.E.I. Management. I'm doing a lot of work with the XYZ, ABC, and 123 companies in the area of cold calling. The reason I'm calling you today specifically is that I just came back from a sales meeting where I learned about the success we've been having in the Philadelphia area. I'd like to stop by next Tuesday at 3:00 and just tell you about our success with other companies in the Philadelphia area."

This allows you to tailor your call to the city in which the prospect resides. Whatever works—whatever you need!

You can also apply this approach to specific kinds of businesses:

> "Good morning, Mr. Jones, Steve Schiffman from D.E.I. Management. We're a sales training firm that does work with firms like Acme Widget and Widget Co. The reason I'm calling you today specifically is that I've been very successful in showing them ways they can increase their widget sales. What I'd like to do is stop by next Tuesday at 3:00 and tell you about the success we've had with those companies."

Once again—I'm not saying that I can do for them what I've done before. I'm simply saying that I've done it for somebody else, and therefore it makes sense for us to get together. This method is utterly different from the approach most salespeople take. Typically, a salesperson calls up and says, "Good morning, Mr. Jones, Jack Smith here from ABC Widgets. The reason I'm calling today is that we have ways we can save you money."

Well, you're not sure of that yet. You don't know anything about this person's business!

"We have ways that can make you more efficient."

You're not sure of that yet, either!

"We have something that could help you."

You're not sure of anything yet!

When you pretend you're sure about how you can help the person, all you do is create a response in kind that allows the other person to say, "Well, I don't know whether you can really do that. That's not right for us."

That means you now have to defend yourself. What a waste of everyone's time and energy!

Still, suppose you take a completely wrong approach for some reason. Suppose you do get sidetracked because the person responds: "Well, you've just said you do X, and here are 12 great, detailed reasons X will never work for us."

You know what to say, don't you? Of course you do.

"Oh, no kidding! Mr. Jones, I'm just curious, what is it that you do?"

Regardless of the way you opened the conversation, his or her answer will give you the Ledge that will enable you to turn the conversation around.

Or suppose you don't get a detailed objection or a direct question (two situations where the Ledge is extremely effective). Suppose you hear:

> *Mr. Jones:* Well, you know, we're really happy with our long distance company. We have no interest in changing.

You can then say:

> *You:* Gee, I've got to tell you, a lot of people we work with have said the same thing before they had a chance to see how what we do complements what they're presently doing.

Or if you hear:

> *Mr. Jones:* Well, I don't know, why don't you send me some literature.

You can say:

> *You:* Oh, Mr. Jones, can't we just get together? How about next Tuesday at 3:00?

Don't defend yourself. Anticipate the responses, use the techniques I've taught you, and *ask for the appointment.*

There are variations on the third-party approach. I know someone who is a very successful life insurance agent. He calls people and says, "Good morning, Mr. Smith, this is Mike Jones from the XYZ Life Insurance Agency. Have you heard of us?"

Inevitably people say "no." Then he says:

> "Oh, well, let me tell you why I'm calling you specifically. I am an agent with the XYZ Life Insurance Agency. We've been very successful working with small business owners in Boston, and what I'd like to do is stop by next Tuesday at 3:00 and just tell you about the success we've had with other small business owners."

Often, the people will say they have life insurance. Then he says, "Oh. Just out of curiosity, are you with ABC Insurance?" The prospect corrects him. (Good salespeople *love* getting corrected.)

> *Mike:* No, we're not with them, we're with Brand X Insurance.

> *Mr. Smith:* Oh, then we really should get together, because I can show you some ways we can complement that program. By the way, have you done any kind of estate planning?

And then, no matter what the answer is, he says, "Oh, that's great. Then we *should* get together. What about next Friday at 3:00?"

I'm not going to tell you that he gets an appointment every time. But the fact is he has become one of the most successful agents in the entire country by using the third-party approach and the Ledge.

Referral Calls

You can use the referral call when you have called someone in the organization, and that person has referred you to someone else. This approach helps you make the most of that opportunity to get an appointment.

Now you already know that when you telephone somebody and that person says, "I'm the wrong person to speak with," you're not going to ask, "Okay, who's the right person?" Instead, you're going to say, "Oh, what do you do?"

This is where you have to be ready to think on your feet. Sometimes, you'll realize you really *are* speaking to the wrong person. Sometimes, you'll ask the person you're talking to for an appointment.

Assume you're able to confirm that you really are dealing with someone who is the wrong person. Assume too, that you ask your contact for the name of the right person to meet with.* Usually the contact will say something like "Why don't you get in touch with Pete Smith."

How should you use that information? Most salespeople call and say the following.

---

* I prefer to ask, "Who would I be meeting with?" rather than "Who handles so-and-so?" At this point in the call you've shared some information about your company with the person and (this is important) asked what he or she does. If you keep the discussion on a personal, one-on-one level, you may get better information.

> "Good morning, Mr. Smith, this is Joe Johnson from XYZ Company here in New York. The reason I'm calling you is that I just spoke to John Jones, and he suggested that I call you and tell you about the work that we're doing. He thought you'd be interested in knowing more about my company."

Don't do it!

Instead, use what you've already figured out. You call Mr. Jones; he tells you he's the wrong person. You get the name of the right person, then you call him. Call the right person and say:

> "Hello, Mr. Smith. This is Jane Smith from XYZ Company here in New York. We're one of the top three widget companies in America. The reason I'm calling you today specifically is that I just spoke to John Jones. He suggested that I give you a call to set up an appointment. I wanted to know if next Tuesday at 3:00 would be okay."

You don't need to go through a full explanation. All you need to say is that your referrer suggested you give a call to set up an appointment. If you follow the system I've set up, your statement will be completely aboveboard. You will have asked for the name of the *person you'd be meeting with*.

At some point in my conversation with Pete Smith you're going to get a reaction. The typical reaction is, "Oh? Why would he want me to meet you? Well, what's this about?" Of course, Pete Smith doesn't know anything about why you're calling.

You can then take a step back and say, "Well, the reason I called John initially was that I had just worked with the XYZ Company. We were very successful in training their salespeople to be more effective on the phone. And when I told him that, he said that I should talk to you to set up an appointment."

Now the person has to react. He can react by saying, "Well, we don't do anything like that." To which you're going to say (you know it already, right?), "Oh. So what do you do?" And no matter what he says next, you're going to say, "Well, you know something, we *should* get together. How about next Thursday at 3:00?" So even with a referral call, we can still use the response turnarounds and the Ledge effectively.

The Ledge, I cannot overemphasize, is the technique you must, without fail, become familiar with. I tell salespeople to take a piece of paper or an index card, write the word "Ledge" on it, and keep it in front of them at all times when they make calls. Use the Ledge just as I've outlined it in this book!

You can use the referral approach in any number of situations. I recently met someone in Cincinnati who told me that I ought to call a friend of his in Indianapolis. I called the friend and said: "Hi, I met with so-and-so in Cincinnati and he suggested I call and set up an appointment for us to get together. I'm going to be in Indianapolis next week." (This was, in fact, the case.)

It worked—and we got a significant account from that visit!

CHAPTER 8

Leaving Messages
That Get Results

I'm always a little bit mystified when I run into salespeople who tell me they "don't believe" in voice-mail messages when it comes to making prospecting calls. Nowadays, that's a little bit like saying you don't believe in the planet Earth.

All the same, there are a good many salespeople we train who swear that it's a waste of time to leave messages for prospects. I have a sneaking suspicion that these salespeople simply don't like making prospecting calls in the first place. Reaching someone's voice-mail box is common now. Excluding all those potential contacts is, I think, basically a rationalization for the bad idea of focusing your calling efforts on "warm calls" to people who are already familiar to you. The problem is, there usually aren't enough people in that category to support your revenue goals.

Let's face it: A huge number of decision-makers use voice mail to screen virtually all of their calls. Why would you want to simply hand that group of potential customers over to the competition?

I also talk to a lot of salespeople who take the opposite approach. They overcall cold contacts, and leave two, three, five, or even more voice-mail messages per week. All that time, effort, and potential annoyance for people who have not yet set any kind of Next Step!

This method of using voice mail is not only a huge waste of time, but also a poor way to initiate a business relationship. Think back on the last time you received three or more consecutive voice-mail messages in a single week from someone you didn't know. Were you more or less likely to return the person's calls at the end of the week?

There's another potential danger with abusing voice-mail systems in this way when reaching out to new contacts: You may be tempted to distort your own calling numbers, and that can make identifying correct ratios and targets difficult. I can't tell you the number of salespeople I've worked with who've informed me that they make "fifty calls a week," but who actually make calls to just 10 new contacts over a five-day period. They leave a message a day for each of those contacts, and consider each of those messages to be a separate call!

In this book, when I talk about making a certain target number of prospecting calls per day, I'm talking about reaching out to—and, if necessary, leaving voice-mail messages for—X number of brand-new people you haven't tried to reach in any way, shape, or form that week. That's the standard to use. It implies, of course, that you should leave no more than one voice-mail message per business week when trying to establish connection with a new contact.*

On the whole, I've found that good salespeople actually prefer delivering a solid, professional message to a voice-mail system, and dealing with the resulting return call. Here are five reasons for that.

---

* The situation is different, of course, once you've established some kind of Next Step with the person in question. At that point, you're dealing with an active prospect; it's quite common for people with busy schedules to exchange three or four messages before connecting in person or by phone, and some business relationships will actually unfold almost exclusively by means of voice mail or some other messaging option. The point is, there's a different standard once you've gotten the contact to agree to meet with you in person.

1. The dynamic of the call is likely to be much more favorable, and a conversational tone will often be much easier to achieve.
2. When the person calls back, you're somewhat less likely to be interrupted (because you're less likely to be perceived as an interruption).
3. When the person calls back, he or she is more likely to actually listen to what you have to say.
4. You can easily leave messages for people who are difficult or impossible to reach directly on the phone.
5. You can make prospecting calls to voice-mail systems at just about any time of the day or night, which gives you more flexibility in scheduling.

In the age of voice mail, you must know how to leave a message that can increase your chances of having the person get back to you. I'm going to give you two specific, very effective ways to leave a message. The first way will give you between 65 and 75 percent return calls. The second way is almost 99 percent effective!

Calling with a Company Name

Here's the first way, the way that most representatives we train leave messages.

Let's say I'm calling someone, and the secretary or receptionist tells me I'm going to have to leave a message. If you recall the phone scripts from earlier chapters, the central reason for my calling is the success I had with the XYZ Company. Therefore, my referring comment or my reference point should be the XYZ Company. So my message will sound like this:

> "This is Steve Schiffman from D.E.I. Management; my telephone number is 212-555-1234. Would you please tell him it's in reference to the XYZ

Company?" Or, for a voice-mail system: "This is
Steve Schiffman from D.E.I. Management; my phone
number is 212-555-1212. It's regarding XYZ
Company."

So when he or she calls me back, I'm going to say: "Oh, I'm
glad you called me. The reason I called you is that we recently
did a project with the XYZ Company."

And then I immediately go into my call about being successful with the XYZ Company. I have to carry that through. If
I don't, then the calls will not be consistent.

You can't lie or mislead. You must leave your company's
name as well as the referring company's. You must be precise,
and you must make sure that the secretary or the assistant gets
the name of your company. Be careful *not* to give the impression that you represent the XYZ Company. If you do that, you
will have trouble later on. Maybe not on your first call or your
second call, but eventually someone's going to say you misled
them, and they'll be right.

The interesting thing is, you don't have to use a huge company for this strategy to work. It doesn't matter whether or
not the person even knows the company, as long as you get
him or her on the phone. You can use a company that you're
familiar with or a company that your contact should be
familiar with, but isn't. If the person says to you, "Well, I don't
know anything about the XYZ Company," you can start by
saying, "Oh, well they're the biggest widget company in the
area. They do A, B, and C. Anyway, the reason I was calling
you . . ." and then you can go right into your opening.

It doesn't even matter if the person tells you that he doesn't
really care about that company, because now you're on the
phone together. You can say, "Oh, that's all right. I'm just
curious, though. What do you do?" And you're going to use
their answer to create the Ledge for yourself. So it doesn't
really matter how people respond to the message you leave,

whether that response is positive or negative—as long as they call you back.

We get between 65 and 75 percent of our calls returned using this method.

Calling with an Individual's Name

The second method of leaving a message came to me in an interesting way.

Every once in a while, it's necessary to terminate someone; sometimes people just leave. That's just the way things go. Some time ago I had a representative working for me who didn't work out—I'm going to call him Bob Jones. After Bob left the company, I started thinking that, as president, I really should call everybody Bob had ever talked to in order to see whether I could start the conversation again.

The first company I called was a huge telecommunications company that Bob had met with; the headquarters were not far from our office in Manhattan. I asked to speak to the president of the company; the secretary got on the phone and said to me, "I'm sorry, he's busy. What's it in reference to?" Now remember, I usually say that my name is Steve Schiffman, my company is D.E.I. Management Group, my telephone number is . . . and I go on to mention the referring company. But in this case, I had Bob Jones on my mind. I had been thinking about him for some time, because it was a little bit frustrating to me that he hadn't worked out. So I simply said that Bob Jones was my reason for calling. The secretary took the message.

About 20 minutes later, the president of the company called me back and said, "You had called me in reference to Bob Jones."

I said, "Oh, yes. Bob Jones worked for our company a number of weeks ago. He's no longer with us, and the reason I was calling you today is we've been very successful working with the ABC Bank. I'd like to stop by next Tuesday at 3:00 and tell you about our success with them."

He gave me the appointment, and we eventually started a business relationship.

I started thinking about that, about how many other people Bob had met with. And so I called everybody and nearly every single person—almost 100 percent—called me back. I used the same message every time, referring to Bob Jones. Now, I don't know whether or not they really remembered Bob Jones, nor do I care. I never asked that question. And when I showed up for an appointment, sometimes he would come up in conversation, and sometimes he wouldn't. But they virtually all called me back. So I asked myself: How else can I use this approach?

Maria, a sales rep who's been with us for about a year, was very frustrated because she had gone on a major sales call, and the person she had met with decided to stop returning her calls. I called her contact's office. Here's how the conversation went:

Steve: Can I speak to Brian Smith?

Secretary: I'm sorry. He's busy right now. What's it in reference to?

Steve: No problem. My name is Steve Schiffman. My company is D.E.I. Management Group. My number in New York is 212-555-1234. Would you please tell him it's in reference to Maria. (And I gave Maria's last name.)

Thirty-five minutes later he called me back.

Customer: You called me in reference to Maria?

Steve: Yes, you had met with Maria a number of months ago.

Customer: Oh, yes.

Steve: Anyway, I wanted to find out what happened.

And he told me the story. I found out that the sale was over, but the fact is I got him on the phone in under an hour. (Maria had told me that was impossible.)

My point is, you can use this technique in a lot of different situations. Have your manager call contacts at those organizations where the sale did not happen. Remember, the status quo is your number one competitor. If that's true, and it is, then the odds are that your contact did nothing after your visit. So, therefore, your manager can say:

> "Mr. Jones, I understand that you worked with Jan Smith, one of our representatives, and nothing really happened. I just wanted to know if there was something that we did wrong."

In other words, your boss should make the assumption that your organization did something wrong. That's a lot better than saying the prospect did something wrong! Virtually every time, this is what your sales manager will hear:

> *Prospect:* Oh, no, Jan was great! It's just that we had these three problems, A, B, and C.

Your boss can then say:

> *Manager:* Oh, then we *should* get together, because we've been working with other companies who've had the same situation. How about next Tuesday at 3:00?

Working as a Team

Another way to use this technique is for two reps to trade off names. We have a number of salespeople in our office who do this. Ross will make the initial call. Sometimes, for whatever reason, he does not get through, and the person he's trying to reach doesn't call him back. Now, Melody uses Ross's name to call. Her message will be, "This is Melody from D.E.I. calling in reference to Ross."

This is all perfectly legitimate. Ross *had* called, and the contact never called him back. We don't know why not. When she gets the prospect on the phone, Melody simply says, "Ross from our office had called you. I'd like to stop by."

Typically, they'll call back and she'll get the appointment. So does Ross. But he does it in reverse, using Melody's name. You can use this method with your colleagues, or your manager can work with you.

There are many different ways to use this technique. For example, you can call all of the companies that other representatives in your company have called and have not been successful with.

Let's say two years ago Jimmy Jones picked up the phone and called the Umbrella Company of America. He never got through. You want to call again. Simply use Jimmy Jones's name in your message:

> "Hi, would you please tell him I called? My name is Chris Smith from the XYZ Company. My phone number is 555-1212. Would you please tell him it's in reference to Jimmy Jones."

When the prospect calls back, you're going to say:

> "Hi, you had spoken to Jimmy Jones from my company a number of years ago. The reason I'm calling is that we've been very successful with the ABC Widget Company. I'd like to stop by . . ."

The strategy I've outlined makes it easy to get return calls almost 100 percent of the time, and it virtually eliminates problems with gatekeepers.

Every once in a while, a secretary asks me what my call is in reference to. I simply reply that it's a long story. If pressed, I ask the secretary whether he or she wants to hear the whole story. Most secretaries say no.

I always leave a message, either with a human being or a voice-mail system.

If They Still Don't Call Back . . .

I do not persist in calling people after a certain point. My approach is simply that once I've called, I assume you're going to call me back. If I don't hear from you within a week or so, my assumption is you didn't get the message, and I'm going to call you again. As a general rule, I make no more than four attempts to contact a decision-maker at a particular company in a given month. You should follow the same rule.

I meet salespeople who say, "Steve, I call a hundred people a week." In reality, they call 10 people 10 times each. That may add up to a hundred, but really it's a very different number.

Years ago, a salesperson at a major company told me that she had called a decision-maker over 400 times, and still had not gotten an appointment! That's like calling somebody 15 times a day, every single day, for a month straight. Why would anybody do that?

Dealing with Telephone Tag

Telephone tag has to be the scourge of all salespeople. We call somebody over and over again; they call us, but we can't seem to connect. How do you handle that?

Salespeople face this obstacle every day. We probably won't reach up to one-third of all the people we actually call simply because they didn't answer the phone. They're busy, or they're away, or they are in a meeting. You trade calls back and forth. This can be very frustrating.

My whole approach to appointment-making is based on the assumption that the prospect and I ought to get together. After all, why would I doubt that? So I'm going to use that assumption in dealing with telephone tag problems.

I've called the prospect, I've expressed interest in our getting together, and in making an appointment to meet. The prospect has also expressed some interest. Whether or not this person directly said, "I'm interested," the contact has *not* said to me, "No, I'll never see you," or, "No, never call me again." Once in a great while you do get such a response, but let's be realistic. Most people respond—in kind—by either saying, "No, this is not the best time," or by making an appointment.

What's really happening in telephone tag? The problem is that you have not really connected with a prospect. If you do connect, then you're going to set up a meeting. But do you really have to connect, or can you simply use the resources at hand to set the appointment?

Consider this sample call:

Steve: Mr. Jones, the reason I'm calling you is to set an appointment.

Mr. Jones: Please call me back.

I call Mr. Jones back in three weeks or in six months, depending on what his time frame is. What do I say? Listen:

Steve: Mr. Jones, the reason I'm calling you specifically is that when we spoke in May you suggested I give you a call today to set up an appointment. Would next Tuesday be okay?

That's a highly effective follow-up call. Use it! (By the way much more about follow-up calls appears in Chapter 9.)

But let's say that, for whatever reason, I *don't* get to talk to Mr. Jones when I call back, so I leave the following message on Mr. Jones's voice mail.

> "Hi, Mr. Jones—Steve Schiffman here from D.E.I. The reason I called is that when we spoke in May you suggested I call today to set up an appointment. I looked in my schedule and I see that I'm going to be in Philadelphia next Thursday, and I wanted to know if next Thursday at 2:30 is okay. My number is 212-555-1234."

That's the entire call. The approach uses the assumption that this person and I are in fact going to get together. (Again: Why *not* assume that?) This approach can be used with voice mail or with a secretary. You and the prospect have simply missed each other.

So refer to your first call in your follow-up call. (Never skip the first call or make untrue statements about whether you've called in the past.) Give a reason to set the appointment that day—because you're going to be in Philadelphia. (Never say, "I'm going to be in the neighborhood." That makes it sound like you're driving around Philadelphia with time on your hands. I don't think that's the message you want to send!)

Be specific. Say, "I'm going to be in Philadelphia next Thursday. I'm meeting with the XYZ Company. I could see you at 2:00, is that okay?" That kind of call will get a better response. Anything specific you can add usually gets a better response: "I'm going to be in Los Angeles a week from Friday to see the XYZ Company. Could we get together right after that?"

That's the kind of call you want to make. It sounds professional, organized, and respectful.

g Messages

how you how to use this method *without* any previous
's say that I'm calling a company that I want to do busi-
. For whatever reason, the contact is not taking my call.
he's not interested. If that's so, I want to know that.
ust simply call up and say, "Hi, this is Steve Schiffman,"
ther I've reached voice mail or a secretary doesn't matter.
 message should sound something like this:

> "This is Steve Schiffman. I just looked at my schedule. I
> realize I'm going to be in Philadelphia next week to
> see the XYZ Company. I'll be about 20 minutes
> from your place. I'd like to get together. Would next
> Thursday about 2:30 work out?"

Now the person has to react—you've put the ball in his
court. He's got to deal with you, either by making an
appointment or not making an appointment. Obviously,
you're *not* going to go over unless the person agrees to see
you. And I'm not suggesting that you go on an appointment
simply for the sake of putting mileage on your car. I am
saying, though, that you can often set up a good appointment
through voice mail or by leaving a message with a secretary
using the strategies I've outlined.

Suppose you've just set up your first appointment in
Philadelphia. You can think to yourself, "Okay, now that I've
set up this appointment in the Philadelphia area, why don't I
begin to set up *more* meetings for Philadelphia?" Now you can
call all the prospects you have in Philadelphia, all the people
that you're talking with in Philadelphia, and all the people
you've ever called or anybody in your office has ever called in
Philadelphia. Use the methods I've given you to make those
calls and set up more appointments.

Now your calls sound like this:

"I'm going to be in Philadelphia, let's get together."

Suddenly you have a good reason to call a prospect back. You have a reason to make follow-up calls. You can now set up a major sales effort in Philadelphia!

Telephone tag problems are easy to solve if you understand the big concept: The person has asked you to call back and, therefore, you're calling back. You don't necessarily have to speak to the individual directly—you can simply set the appointment.

Sometimes it's easier to understand this process by looking at the entire sequence of events. Consider this series of calls, for instance.

The first time I call, I don't get through, so I leave a message: "Hi, this is Steve Schiffman. I'm calling in reference to Jim Jones." Or, "I'm calling in reference to XYZ Company."

Either way, the person calls me back. If I miss the call because I'm busy going on appointments, I call the person back again. Now they call me back. So: I've called them, they've called me; I've called them, they've called me. On the third call I leave my message:

> "Hi, Mr. Jones, this is Steve Schiffman. The reason I was calling you is to set an appointment. Would next Tuesday at 2:00 be okay?"

Again, I can do this either with voice mail or I can do it with a secretary. I can use the same message if I happen to get through to the person I want to talk to. The fact is, I've shortened my message. I don't need to leave a longer message because I've already called. My *assumption* is that the prospect is going to see me, so I ask: "Can we get together next Tuesday at 2:00?"

This is the single best way to defeat telephone tag. It's breathtaking in its simplicity. And it works!

A Few Words about E-Mail

I'm not a big proponent of trying to use e-mail messages to initiate business relationships; I think telephone prospecting is still the most immediate, direct, and effective strategy for developing prospects. We have, however, had some success in using e-mail to support and expand existing business relationships.

Given the extraordinary popularity of this medium of communication, a few notes on how to get the most of it—based simply on personal experience, and not on any formal research—are probably in order.

Expect people to delete messages from people they don't know. You do it, I do it, everyone does it. If the sender is unfamiliar, the instinct can be overwhelming for us to hit "delete" rather than examine a message that appears to have nothing whatsoever to do with us. There is some room for experimentation here, of course, but I would not recommend spending vast amounts of time tracking down individual e-mail addresses and sending hopeful messages out to them. I would also advise against purchasing lists of addresses and conducting mass e-mail campaigns, for the simple reason that more and more people today deeply resent receiving unwanted e-mail from total strangers. Any number of online entrepreneurs could give you different advice, of course, but my focus has always been on initiating profitable business relationships, and e-mail blitzes don't seem to me to be a great way of doing that.

Use e-mail to maintain a distinct, personal connection with current clients, prospects, and customers. Once you've established a reciprocal relationship with someone, e-mail can be an extremely important sales tool. There are, of course, people who use e-mail as a primary business communication method. That means that, for a good portion of your contact base, e-mail will be *essential* in setting up Next Steps, getting feedback on ideas, and conducting follow-through efforts.

Make the message easy to take action on. That means keeping your note relatively short (preferably readable in full without having to "page down"). It also means getting right to the point and establishing a clear goal for the future that benefits both parties. For instance:

> Hi! It was a real pleasure meeting with you and Dave today; I'm attaching a copy of the specifications you asked for. I'd like to get your feedback on how this looks before our group meeting on the eleventh.
> I'm going to plan on calling you on Monday at 2:00—can you let me know if this is a good time?
> Sincerely,
> Jeff

Use subject lines that focus clearly on the Next Step you have in mind. Boring or poorly constructed subject headings can keep your message from even being opened; subject headings that focus on the action you have in mind will usually win attention and a quick return e-mail. For instance, in the message above, a subject line that read "Specification documents" would probably be ignored entirely, or put off to be "opened later." On the other hand, a subject line that read "Upcoming call: Monday, June 25th at 2:00" would certainly get your contact's attention—and, more than likely, a spot on the person's calendar, which is what you're after.

One final warning on e-mail messages is in order: Take advantage of the informality of the medium if you wish, but don't let your message get too casual. It is easier than you might imagine to send an inappropriate e-mail note. This is, I think, because it is so easy to compose "on the fly" and hit "send" without reviewing the message carefully and double-checking for important details (like the spelling of someone's name). Play it safe: Look your message over closely before you send it, and delete or revise any portion that could possibly be offensive. Better yet, compose your message in a word processor, edit and double-check it to your heart's content, and then paste it into your e-mail messaging system when it's time to send it. That way, you'll be able to spell-check and grammar-check the message before it goes out.

CHAPTER 9

Follow-Up Calls

Follow-up calls are what you make when someone asks you to call back in order to set an appointment.

For example, I call up John Jones and ask for an appointment, using one of the script formats in this book. But Mr. Jones says to me, "Steve, I'd love to talk to you but I'm really busy right now." So I use my turn-arounds by saying to him, "Other people have said the same thing . . ." or "Can't we just get together next Thursday. . . ." But he insists, saying, "Look, I'm very busy right now, and this is simply not the best time. You're going to have to call me back in the fall."

There are always going to be people who won't want to talk to you. Please remember: We're not looking to get every appointment, although we'd like to get every single appointment where we have a reasonable chance of doing so.

With follow-up calls, the objective is simply to build our competitive edge—to improve our ratio of success.

When the prospect says, "You're going to have to call me back," I assume that when I do call him back, I'm going to talk with him to *set the appointment*. That's an important point. I'm not calling him back next Thursday because I have nothing else to do. I'm calling him back because he asked me to call him back when I first called him to set up an appointment.

Remember That People Respond in Kind

The only way that you can accept this premise is if you remember that people respond in kind. After all, I said to him, "The reason I'm calling you is to set an appointment." Then he said to me, "Steve, I'm busy right now. You'll have to call me back." My assumption, unless I hear otherwise from him, is that I should call back *to set the appointment*. After all, that's what he is responding to. That's what I've asked for. So that's what I'm basing the follow-up call on. Look at it again:

> "Good morning, Mr. Jones, this is Steve Schiffman from the XYZ Widget Company here in Madison, Wisconsin. The reason I'm calling you today specifically is that, when we spoke last June, you suggested I give you call today in September to set up an appointment. Would next Tuesday at 3:00 be okay?"

This is very different from what most salespeople do. Most salespeople do this:

> "Good morning, Mr. Jones, this is Steve Schiffman from the XYZ Widget Company here in Madison, Wisconsin. When I called you a while back, I explained that I worked with the 1234 Company. You were interested at the time but you said it wasn't a good time. So I'm calling you now and I just wanted to know if you might be interested in the possibility of hearing more about us."

I can't say it enough: People respond in kind! This opening is begging for a response like, "No, I'm not interested," or, "No, I'm too busy." But it's extremely easy to make that call! It takes practice to make a better call. This is why your scripts and your choice of words are so important. This is why we teach people to tape-record themselves making calls so that they can listen in on the calls and improve on their mistakes. I've recorded a number of people during role plays at our training programs. Once these people hear their own tapes, they understand why they haven't been getting appointments.

If you start in with, "The reason I'm calling you is that we had spoken a long time ago and you had expressed some interest then and I wanted to see if now is a better time," all you're doing is encouraging the person to say, "No, it's not a better time." Guess what? It will *never* be a better time!

Here's one more example of what your call should sound like:

> "Good morning, Mr. Jones, this is Steve Schiffman from XYZ Widget Company here at Anytown, USA. The reason I'm calling you today specifically is when we spoke in June, you suggested I give you a call today (you can mention the date if it's appropriate to do so) to set an appointment. Would next Tuesday be okay?"

Now the person has to respond to you. (Does that sound familiar? Good!) You know the person's going to respond to you. In fact, you're prepared for the response. The person could say:

> "Well, Steve, the fact is this is still not a good time to talk. I'm really busy right now."

As an expert cold caller, you now understand how you're going to work with this response.

You're going to create a Ledge by saying something like this:

> "Gee, Mr. Jones, I'm just curious, what are you doing now? Who are you using for your widgets?"

The person will respond to you. They'll say something like: "We're using Acme widgets. And you know what? We're really happy with what we've got."

If you know your competition, you might decide to respond by saying, "Gee, are you using the Red Velvet model or the Blue Velvet model?" Then the person might say, "Neither. We're using the Green Velvet one."

You can then say, "Oh, that's great! You know something, we really *should* get together. We really complement Green Velvet very well. How's Friday at 3:00?"

Give it a shot, even though you know you're not going to get an appointment every time. But I guarantee you that at least 10 percent of those people you talk to during follow-up calls are going to see you. And that's 10 percent that you would not have gotten otherwise.

When to Call Back

As to *when* to call somebody back, I don't like to give someone three months, six months, or a year before I call them back. I think that's foolishness. And yet—how do you break down that time barrier? What reason do you use for calling earlier? There are probably a million reasons you can call people back. Here's my favorite:

"I was just thinking about you yesterday."

Not long ago, I was teaching salespeople at a major telecommunications company. The company was going through a major merger at that point. I told everyone in the room that they should pick up the phone on Monday morning and call every single person they were supposed to call back at any point in the next three months.

I asked them to say something along these lines:

"Good morning, Mr. Jones, this is Steve Schiffman from Data International Company here in Blank,

Texas. The reason I'm calling you is that I was thinking about you yesterday. We were at a national sales meeting where I learned about a major merger that now puts us in a unique position, and I'd like to get together to tell you about some of the new things I've just learned."

The results? A lot more appointments!

The key to any call like that is the phrase, "I was just thinking about you yesterday." People respond to that, of course, and they're usually quite positive. I've had people say to me, "No kidding! I was thinking about you, too." Or, "It's a funny thing you called, we were thinking about doing X." Whatever the person says, the point is that you now have a reason to call, and you've eliminated that three-month waiting time.

I'm working with a company right now that I'd once had great difficulty getting business from. When I called I was told, "Why don't you call me back after the summer?" Of course, I didn't wait until after the summer. I called back 30 days later, and the call went like this.

Steve: You know something, I was driving past a building, and I looked up and saw a billboard that advertised one of your products, and I thought of you, and I thought I'd give you a call.

That's all I said. My contact came right back with:

Prospect: You know something, I was actually thinking about *you* the other day.

Steve: No kidding?

Prospect: Yes.

Steve: You know what, we should get together.

Prospect: Sure, come on in.

And that did it. Eventually, I got that business.

Do you understand the concept behind this approach? Your opening line is, "I was just thinking about you," which is absolutely true. Even if you weren't thinking about the person before you made the call, calling will certainly make you think about that person!

Once you start to think about it, you'll realize you can use this approach for almost any call you want to make. You can call anybody up and say:

> "You know, I was looking through my list and I was thinking about you."

> "You know, I just happened to be in Jackson, Mississippi, yesterday. I was thinking about you."

> "You know, I was driving on Interstate 88 the other day and I was thinking about you. I'm going to be in Indiana; I thought we could get together. "

This brings us to another approach you can use for follow-up calls. Consider this true story. Looking at my schedule recently, I saw that I was going to be in New Albany, Indiana. New Albany, Indiana, is a very small town outside of Louisville, Kentucky. The point is that I was going to go to New Albany, Indiana, because I was visiting a client there. I called somebody who's in Atlanta, Georgia, and I said, "You know something, I was looking at my schedule the other day, and I realized I'm going to be in New Albany, Indiana, next Thursday and I thought maybe we should get together on Friday." And my contact said, "Okay, that makes sense."

Not much later, I used the same technique again! I called somebody in Texas. He said to me, "Look, I'm really busy this week. I can't see you." So I said, "Gee, I'm just looking at my schedule. On the 13th (which was about two weeks from that day), I'm going to be in Charlotte, North Carolina." Do you realize that Dallas and Charlotte are nowhere near each other? But that's what I said. "I'm going to be in Charlotte, North Carolina. I have to give a speech there. Why don't we get together the day before?" He said, "Okay." And all of a sudden there's a reason to meet. Somehow it makes sense. You're closer than you were before. If your budget accommodates this strategy, give it a try.

Build Up Your Arsenal!

You can use all of these methods to make your calls. Use everything you can. Develop your arsenal of cold calling techniques. For my part, I will call a prospect for every reason I can possibly think of. The sun's up; the sun's down. It's been a good day; it's been a bad day. Just made a sale; just lost a sale. Closed the deal; opened the deal. It doesn't matter. Every single event gives me an opportunity to call, start the conversation, and reduce the waiting time before the actual meeting.

And if the follow-up call doesn't go smoothly right off the bat, you know what to do: *create the Ledge!*

CHAPTER 10

The Four-Step Sales Process

Now that we've taken a thorough look at cold calling and the various ways of setting appointments, let's look at how what you've learned fits into the overall sales process. There are basically four stages to the sales process:

- The Opening
- The Information Stage
- The Presentation Stage
- The Closing Stage

One of the questions I ask salespeople when I conduct my seminars is "What's the objective of the first step?" The discussion usually goes like this:

Salesperson: Well, Steve, the objective of the first step is to meet somebody, to greet them, to create rapport.

Steve: No, that's not it.

Salesperson: Well, it has to be. You haven't built up any rapport yet.

Steve: Sorry. That's not it.

Salesperson: Okay, it's to create a first impression. It's to contact them.

Steve: That's not it either.

Salesperson: Then the objective is to get the person to pick up the phone.

Steve: Nope.

And on it goes. What is the objective of the first step? *The objective of the first step is simply to get to the next step.*

Similarly, the objective of the second step is to get to the third. The objective of the third step is to get to the fourth. If you look at it that way, what you realize is that when you're completing each step, you're getting closer to your goal of closing the sale. Since the status quo is your number one enemy, and time is so important, your objective is always to advance the sale as efficiently as you can.

Advance the Sale

You're always looking for ways to advance the sale. That means the only way you know your meeting was good or bad was *whether or not you got to the next step*. The fact that you sat down and talked to somebody, or that the person said to you, "This is a great meeting; this is wonderful" means absolutely nothing if you don't move to the next step.

When I go on first appointments, I know my objective is to get to the next step: to come back for a second appointment. The success of these sales meetings is determined by whether or not I'm going to come back, *not* on how I felt the meeting went.

So: There are certain steps in the sales process. The last step, the close, comes from the third step, which is the presentation.

The presentation comes from the second step, which is the information step. And of course, the information step comes from the first step, the opening. Let's take a quick look at how the sequence moves forward. (For a more in-depth discussion of the sales process, see my book *Power Sales Presentations*, published by Adams Media Corporation.)

The Opening

I was doing a program for an HMO recently. There were about 100 people in the room. A young man in his early twenties recounted the story of his very first sales call in his first sales job. (Remember what that was like?)

The story goes like this: As he's heading out the door for his first sales call, his manager says, "Look, the first thing you do when you go on an appointment is look at the photographs on the prospect's desk. Look at the photographs, say something about the family, and you'll create rapport." So here he is, 22 years old, on his first day at a new job. He walks into the person's office, who happens to be a 55-year-old senior manager. He goes up to the photographs. He picks up the photographs. They are the four ugliest people he has ever seen in his life.

Not knowing what to do, he turns to the prospect and said, "Mr. Prospect, these are some great looking frames."

Well, of course, we all make mistakes during meetings with prospects. Sometimes we do a product dump on the prospect—telling them everything about our product, probably more than they ever wanted to know, without letting the other person get a word in edgewise. We may even ask a couple of questions that aren't relevant.

Don't use gimmicky openings. Simply get acquainted with the person, one human being to another. Be clear and to the point. Remember, the opening is just to get you to the next step, so this "getting-to-know-you" phase can be relatively spontaneous, short, and sweet. (This idea also translates to your cold call openings, which we've already discussed.)

The Information Stage

In this stage, it's vitally important to ask yourself: What information do I have to know in order to make the right presentation? If you agree that the close comes from the presentation and the presentation comes from the information, you have to determine the information that you must ask about. This is a roundabout way of saying that you can't assume you already have all the answers.

Don't ask people: "What do you need?" Telling people to go and find out what prospects need is one of the most misleading approaches taught in sales today. As you know by now, people *don't* need us, and we shouldn't conduct the interview as though they did.

Remember the one-third sales rule. One-third of your potential sales will fall into your lap. One-third depends on your selling skills. One-third won't go your way. When you're gathering information, you're fighting for that second one-third which is *not* going to fall into your lap. That means your information-gathering cannot be based on needs.

Allow me to repeat this, because it warrants repetition. The real key to successful selling is finding out what people do. If you understand what they do, how they do it, when they do it, where they do it, who they do it with, why they've chosen to do it that way, and whether your product could help them do it better, you're going to be successful. Success comes from helping people do what *they* want to do, not what *you* want to do.

You and I want to make a sale. There's no question about that. If you want to be able to go in and say, "Gee, I can show

you how what I do will help you do what you do better," then
you first have to ask questions that help you understand what
this person does. There are hundreds of such questions, but
since this is a book about cold calling I'll have to content
myself with giving you one of the very best. Here it is: "What
is it you're trying to accomplish here?"

When you have the answer to that (and it will take a while
to get it), you'll be ready for your presentation.

Here's an important rule of thumb: The information-
gathering stage should occupy about 75 percent of your
selling process.

The Presentation Stage

Do you know the difference between a demonstration and a
presentation? The definition of a presentation is relatively
simple. It's presenting your case for why the prospect's
deciding to buy. Most people confuse demonstrations and presentations. They think they're the same thing. They're not.

And by the way, a demonstration is *not* designed to show
you how a product works. It's designed to get a reaction from
you. When I show you how a copier works in a sales setting,
what I'm really looking for from you is some kind of reaction.
The purpose of a *demonstrat*ion is to get information.

The purpose of a *presentation*, on the other hand, is to
close a sale. Too many salespeople are making demonstrations,
calling them presentations, and not closing the sale. Your
demonstration isn't designed to close a sale. The *presentation*
closes the sale. The *demonstration* gives you the information
you need so you can *make* your presentation. Therefore, you
have to understand that the presentation comes from the
second step, the information step, which should incorporate
any demonstration you plan to make.

The Closing Stage

So we've opened, we've gathered our information from the demonstration, and we've made our presentation. Then we go ahead and try to close the sale with one of those gimmicky sure-fire closing techniques you've probably heard about. The puppy dog close, for instance. Do you know what the puppy dog close is? The puppy dog close is when the salesperson comes in and says, "You know what? Let me leave the machine here for a week. You'll fall in love with it. You'll buy it."

Or how about the Ben Franklin close? This is where you draw a line down the middle of a piece of paper and say, "Mr. Prospect, you write down every single reason you should not buy from me. I'm going to write down every reason you should. If I come up with more reasons than you do, I win, and you lose. You've got to buy." Ridiculous, isn't it?

My favorite close comes from a book I read some years ago. The author recommended turning to the prospect and saying, "Mr. Prospect, if you don't buy from me today, I'm going to lose my job." Could you see yourself saying that?

Have you ever heard of the "three devil" close? This is another one of my favorites. The salesperson turns to the prospect and says, "Mr. Prospect, let me tell you a story." The story is about (you guessed it) three devils. One goes to the right, one goes left, and one goes straight ahead. The story rambles on and on and on. It has no point. The salesperson is suddenly supposed to start laughing abruptly, even though the story doesn't make any sense and has no punchline. "Ho, ho, ho." The theory is that the prospect will be so embarrassed for you that the sale will close itself! Can you see yourself doing that? I hope not! But the sad truth is that many salespeople follow this kind of ridiculous advice.

I don't close that way. You don't have to close that way. If you understand what I said before, then you know I open without gimmicks, and I get information based upon what people do, how they do it, when they do it, where they do it, and who they do it with. I make the right presentation because it is based on that information. It's not based on my product or service. I make the right presentation, showing the way in which what I offer can help them do what they do better. And I close simply by saying, "Mr. Prospect, it makes sense to me . . . what do you think?"

That's it. "Makes sense to me; what do you think?" Simple, isn't it? And it's extremely effective—much more effective than any trick close.

Once you start to understand how well this approach works, you'll see that there's a different, more logical, way to approach selling than you've read about in other books.

Most selling systems get all distracted by the opening and closing stages. Actually, the interviewing stage is what everyone should be focusing on. The closing is simply the last step in a logical progression.

If you've handled the other steps of the sale properly, if you haven't made the mistake of presenting before you have enough information, the closing part simply makes sense. It really does make sense (to you and the other person) that you get the sale.

CHAPTER 11

The Principles of Sales Success

My only real concern when it comes to sales training is whether the training I offer helps people make more sales. If it doesn't, then the training really doesn't make any difference. The purpose of sales training is to help people do what they do—that is, sell—better—that is, make more sales.

With that aim in mind, let's look now at some of the basic principles for sales success.

1. All Steps Lead to the Next Step

The only reason you're making a cold call is to get an appointment. The only reason you went on the appointment is to get to the next step in your sale. Your next step could be the second appointment or it could be a close. It doesn't really matter to me what it is, as long as *you* know what it is. Too many salespeople go on appointments without having any idea what their objective for the visit is.

The objective of every step of the sales process is to get to the next step. If what you're doing doesn't get you to the next step, do something else that does!

2. The Difference Between Success and Failure Is 72 Hours

I think each and every one of us has had a great idea that went unattended. We said, "Boy, I ought to write a book about that," or, "That's a great idea for a movie," or, "I should design something that does that better." Then, six months or a year later we see that our idea has actually been implemented by someone else. Well, what happened? The difference was that the other person took action on the idea.

You can read this book, but if you don't begin to *implement* the concepts that we've talked about here within 72 hours, and then maintain the activity for 21 days, *you're not going to be successful.*

People tend to fall back on what they know. And if you don't get started with these concepts within 72 hours, you'll fall back on what you already know, and you'll have missed an opportunity to be far more successful than you are now. Respond immediately! Find something to implement! Take action now!

Changing your selling techniques within 72 hours really is the key to success.

3. All Objections and Responses Can and Should Be Anticipated

Everything that I've ever created in selling has been based on the premise that I can know in advance what a prospect's response will be—that I can learn to predict how people will respond to me during a cold call or in person.

I know, for example, that on a sales call I'm going to be asked certain questions about my training techniques and about how my seminars work. I'm prepared for these questions. I have my answers ready. If I *didn't* prepare an answer, that would be like going on a sales call without a business card. I would never do that. Would you?

4. Follow-Through Is an Integral Part of Sales

I prefer "follow-through" to "follow-up." Don't you? In fact, I very rarely say to anybody, "I'm going to follow up with a telephone call." What I like to say is "I'm going to follow through by calling you next week." In other words, I'm going to follow through on what I've started. I'm going to complete it. I may not make every sale, but I'm going to follow each relationship through as far as I can.

5. You Must Find Out What the Prospect Does

Find out what people do! Ask them what they do, how they do it, when they do it, where they do it, who they do it with, and why they do it that way. Your job is to help them do it better.

6. Prospects Respond in Kind

I've said it throughout this book, and I'll say it again here. People respond to what you're asking, and they respond in kind to *how* you ask. As I've pointed out repeatedly, if you ask, "Do you need my service?" the odds are you're going to hear a "no." If you talk instead about how you can help them do what they do better, you're going to be successful.

This concept of asking the right questions comes from a discussion Socrates and Plato had about pleasing the gods. They concluded that the pious person was the person who pleased the gods; that is, who made the gods happy. I believe that, in order to make the gods happy, we have to ask the question, "What, exactly, will make them happy?" Therefore, to my way of thinking, a pious person is one who asks the key questions.

If you don't ask questions like "What is it that you do?" or "What are you trying to get accomplished?" you will not get the success you deserve.

7. It's Necessary to Ask for the Appointment

One of the biggest mistakes salespeople make is failing to ask for the appointment. I've heard salespeople ask for just about everything *except* an appointment during a cold call. Guess what? They don't get the appointment!

The Four Ps

Let's go beyond the usual list of selling do's and don'ts. In order to become a more successful salesperson, you should concern yourself with four basic areas of knowledge:

- Professional development
- Product malleability
- Presentation skills
- Prospecting

Professional Development

Ninety percent of all salespeople in the United States fail to read one book about improving their sales techniques in a given year. Furthermore, most salespeople will not pay for their own sales training; 90 percent of all sales training is paid for by the employer. Salespeople will pay for their own swimming lessons, quilting lessons, riding lessons, tennis lessons, horseback riding lessons, driving lessons, and (of course) golf lessons, but they won't pay for their own sales training. You may want to give some thought to whether or not you need to sign up for a program that will help you improve your sales skills. (You've already beaten the odds, however, by reading a sales-related book!)

Product Malleability

"Product malleability" means repositioning your product or service to fit your prospect's specific needs.

Remember, the purpose of your product is to help people do what they do better. Strictly speaking, your product doesn't matter as much as your ability to take it and apply it—and that means, of course, that you have to understand your prospect's business. So product malleability comes from your understanding of what your prospect does, and how you can apply what you offer to the prospect's unique situation.

Presentation Skills

Presentation skills account for an important part of your overall success, but they probably aren't as important as you might think at first. Many people practice their presentations constantly, using role-playing, memorization, and even videotaping to hone their "moment" with the prospect. Do they realize that the ratio of calls to appointments is usually three-to-one—and sometimes even higher?

I would be foolish if I told you that making a good presentation to your prospect is not important. But in the overall scheme of things, it is still not as important as getting in the door—prospecting. And, of course, no amount of practice can perfect a presentation that is not based on solid information about the prospect.

Prospecting

Prospecting is really what this book is about. It's what makes the difference. We did a study of successful salespeople making between $75,000 and $125,000 a year consistently for 10 consecutive years. We learned that 45 percent of the success of an individual salesperson comes directly from his or her ability to prospect. Twenty percent comes from presentation skills. Twenty percent comes from product knowledge or product malleability, and the remaining 15 percent comes from sales training. In other words, 65 percent of what successful salespeople do is finding people and talking about potential applications; that's prospecting and presenting combined.

Ten Traits of Successful Salespeople

In all the years that I've traveled and during all the programs I've done, I've given approximately 8,000 speeches and trained about 450,000 salespeople. I've found that there are certain key characteristics that make people successful in sales. Here are the top 10.

1. They're Not Normal.

You've decided to go into sales and, therefore, by the very definition, you're not normal. Sales success is not a normal state. Sales success is not normal—because success means being willing to act differently. When you're successful, you're not normal, and because you're going to maintain that success, you're comfortable with the idea of never being normal again!

2. They're Committed.

Successful salespeople are committed to their goals, and they *have* goals. Not only do you have to be committed to your own goals, but you have to be committed to the goals of your company. Do you understand those goals? Do you understand fully what your company is trying to accomplish?

You're also looking to work with the goals of your customers. As soon as salespeople say to me that they're concerned about their commission checks, then I start worrying whether or not they're concerned about their customers. If you help customers accomplish their goals, if you help them do what they do better, you will never, ever lose.

3. They're Motivated.

Successful salespeople are self-motivated. They know what they have to do and they know how they're going to get there. Interestingly enough, the role of the sales manager in the successful salesperson's career is really minimal. You and I both know what we have to do. We know we have to make calls. We know we have to follow through and do the things you've been reading about in this book each and every day. We know we have to take action. We have to make things happen.

One of my favorite stories is about a great Hollywood literary agent named Swifty Lazar. His actual name was Irving, but everybody in the business called him Swifty. Swifty Lazar died a number of years ago, but in reading about him, one of the things that struck me was that every single morning, he said he would get up and he would look at his calendar and see what was going to happen that day. And if there was nothing that was going to happen, he made something happen every day . . . before lunch! And that's exactly my philosophy—you make something happen every day . . . before lunch. You get an appointment. You make a call. You start some activity. Because the activity you create today is going to give you business down the road.

4. They're Self-Declared.

Being self-declared means that successful salespeople feel good about themselves. Successful salespeople carry themselves well, they talk themselves up, and they understand what it is they have to accomplish and how they're going to get there.

5. They Sacrifice.

If you ever watched the Olympics, or any committed athlete, you realize that an athlete makes tremendous sacrifices.

They make choices each and every day in order to be successful. They understand that the gain is worth the choice that they're going to make.

6. They Delegate.

Successful salespeople also understand how to prioritize and how to get the things they need to do done. They know how to take best advantage of the resources and the people available to them.

7. They're Optimistic.

Successful salespeople are part of the solution and not part of the problem. It's easy to find problems. Anyone can do that. And yet I'll bet the person you remember most in life, the person you consider your mentor (whether it's your parent, grandparent, coach, or a college professor), is the person who helped you find the solutions.

Successful people are believers. They believe the great mission can be accomplished. They not only believe it; they live it.

8. They're Enthusiastic.

I absolutely, positively love doing what I do. The reason I tell you that is that I want you to be enthusiastic each and every day. Every single day, get up as if it were the first day you've ever sold. Do you remember the very first sales call you went on? Remember that anxiety, that nervousness, the adrenaline pumping through your body? It was exciting! Live that excitement every day!

9. They Live Off-Peak.

Successful salespeople don't drive onto the highway at 8:30 A.M. and sit in traffic. They're going earlier, or they're going later. They're not going with everybody else.

They constantly rethink their options. They're not standing in line at noon for a restaurant. They go earlier or later. They're *not* like the woman in New York City I heard of recently who stood in line for an hour and a half . . . to complain about the lines.

10. They're Consistent and Persistent.

Successful salespeople have the focus and the discipline to follow through on their projects and not get bored. Successful salespeople aren't fickle. They have a plan and stick with it.

The Three Most Important Words in Sales

The three most important words in sales today are *obsession, utilization,* and *implementation.*

Obsession

You need to be *obsessed* by what you're doing. You have to be willing to think about your job seven days a week, 24 hours a day.

Utilization

Obsession without discipline results in chaos. If you're not disciplined enough to stay focused, to make the calls, to do what you have to do to reach your goals, you're not going to be successful. Successful people understand how to utilize everything. So take all the material, all the things that you've read in this book, and use as much as you possibly can to become more successful.

Implementation

And finally, we come to implementation. You just have to do it. You have to implement the plan. You have to do the work. If you don't do it, you're not going to be successful.

A Tale of Two Lumberjacks

Two lumberjacks were given axes and told to go into the forest to cut down trees. The first lumberjack went up to his first tree and started to chop away. He chopped all day long without stopping.

The second lumberjack also did his share of chopping and cutting, but at various points during the day, he would stop, walk away, and come back a few minutes later. Meanwhile, the first lumberjack kept working away.

At the end of the day, the lumberjack who worked nonstop, who never stopped working, had cut less wood than the lumberjack who took breaks.

Do you understand what happened?

The lumberjack who took breaks went to sharpen his ax.

The point is that both men were given the same tool, but only one of them learned how to use the tool properly.

We're all given the same tools. We all play on the same field. We all play by the same rules, yet certain people really learn how to use those tools properly. In the end, it's not the playbook that's important, it's the *execution*. Every basketball team, every football team, plays on the same field. What makes one better than the next? It isn't their playbook. It's their execution. What will make you better than the next person? What will give you the success you need? Your *execution*. Your ability to carry out the plan.

A Guarantee

If, after reading this book, you don't agree that it's the best on the market about appointment-making through cold calling, contact me and I'll return your money without question. All I ask is that you develop a draft of your cold calling script, and track the results of your calls for 21 days. Send me your completed script development materials, the call sheets recording the calls you made and their results, and I'll know you gave the program an honest try.

If you send these materials, along with a note expressing your displeasure with your results, I'll write you a check for the full purchase price of the book. The fact is, though, it's absolutely, positively impossible to fail with my method—if you only try.

• • •

In my office, we have regular sales meetings, but they're a little different in one respect from the meetings in many offices. Certainly you've heard the expression, "Have a nice day." Where I work, we don't say that; we say, "Make it a productive day." It reminds us that we're in control of our destiny, that our success or our failure is in our own hands. It's just the same with you.

Make it a productive day!

Sample Scripts

Finally—you're ready to begin.

Almost every product that you buy today has a set of instructions; many even state something along the lines of "use only as directed." I take a slightly different approach on the matter of tinkering with the simple scripts that follow. Certainly you should feel free to adapt them to your own personal style. But do so in keeping with the spirit of the program outlined in the preceding chapters. *Don't* overembellish.

As you look these scripts over, you may find them a little ambitious. They're meant to be. They're simple, and they're direct. That's why they work.

At one of my seminars recently, a group of salespeople expressed some reservations about these scripts. Why were they so aggressive? Where were the probing questions? How were they to "draw the prospects in"?

Their problem, of course, was that they were wasting their time talking to people they should have classified as simple rejections in the first minute of the conversation. And anyway, selling over the phone, is *not* what cold calling is about.

To address the concerns these people raised, I decided to try a little experiment. I sat down one Tuesday and made seven cold calls in a two-hour period. I got through to two people and got one appointment by using one of the scripts reproduced here—word for word. That's 50 percent. I asked the sales manager if he could match that figure using his current methods. He couldn't. When the salespeople finally saw the results of the program, they decided to give it a try.

The salespeople I'm talking about were lucky. They kept an open mind. If you do the same thing, you'll see a marked improvement in your performance.

The scripts outlined here are the basis for the work you're about to undertake. Obviously, as you get more proficient at your phone prospecting work, you'll change a word here and there to fit your own style and requirements. But the same approach applies—and that's the point. You'll stop wasting time by having extended conversations on the phone. You'll be direct in asking for the appointment. You'll know what you're going to say in advance.

When I start my seminars, I usually begin with the sentence, "When God wanted to punish salespeople, he invented the cold call." That actually sums up my feelings, and possibly yours as well, about the cold call. You, and only you, can turn the "curse" into an opportunity—by beginning to use the techniques I've shown you, and the scripts provided here.

Initial Contact Script

Good morning _____, this is _____ from _____. The reason I'm calling you today specifically is so I can stop by and tell you about our new _____ program that increases _____. I'm sure that you, like _____, are interested in _____.

(Positive response).

That's great _____; let's get together. How's _____?

Third-Party Endorsement Script

Good morning _____, this is _____ from _____. (Insert your brief commercial on your company.) The reason I'm calling you today specifically is that we've just completed working on a major project for _____, which was extremely successful in increasing _____. What I'd like to do is stop by next _____ to tell you about the success I had at _____. How's _____?

Referral Script

Good morning _____, this is _____. (Insert your brief commercial on your company.) The reason I'm calling you today specifically is that _____ just suggested I give you a call to set up an appointment. I wanted to know if _____ at _____ would be okay.

Follow-Up Script

Good morning _____, this is _____ from
_____. A number of weeks ago I contacted you, and you
asked me to call you back today to set up an appointment.
Would _____ be good for you?

Live Training Programs Offered by D.E.I. Management Group

Appointment Making

D.E.I.'s *Appointment Making* workshop focuses on getting in front of more prospects by means of effective telephone prospecting.

Thousands of companies worldwide have successfully implemented *Appointment Making* skills, including **Aetna, ExxonMobil, The Los Angeles Times, Nextel Communications, Sprint PCS,** and **Time Warner Cable.**

As a direct result of this workshop, D.E.I. clients have reported increases in sales of as much as 30 percent, and increases in appointments generated from 33 percent to a high of 81 percent.

To learn more about this live training program, call us at (800) 224-2140, or visit *www.dei-sales.com.*

Getting to "Closed" (Prospect Management)

The D.E.I. *Getting to "Closed"* system is a patented, visually driven system for tracking prospects, strategizing forward movement in the sale, and forecasting income accurately.

Thousands of companies worldwide have successfully implemented the *Getting to "Closed"* system, including **Airborne Express, ExxonMobil, Aetna, MCI WorldCom, LexisNexis, Trans Union, Motorola Canada,** and **Chase Bank.**

Companies have reported a range of 20 percent to 40 percent increases in sales revenues as a result of *Getting to "Closed"* system implementation.

To learn more about this live training program, call us at (800) 224-2140, or visit *www.dei-sales.com.*

High Efficiency Selling Skills

The D.E.I. *High Efficiency Selling Skills* workshop introduces the sales process as a series of steps that will lead to a logical "makes sense" close when implemented properly. The premise behind the program is that we, as sellers, need to understand what our prospects do—in order to help them achieve their goals and do it better.

Over 8,000 companies worldwide have successfully implemented the principles in the *High Efficiency Selling Skills* workshop, including **ExxonMobil, Aetna, Motorola, SEKO Worldwide,** and **Nextel Communications.**

As a direct result of the *High Efficiency Selling Skills* workshop, D.E.I. clients have found they will actually present fewer proposals and close a far higher percentage of them—in some cases as high as **80 percent.**

To learn more about this live training program, call us at (800) 224-2140, or visit *www.dei-sales.com.*

Online Training Programs Offered by D.E.I. Management Group

Visit us at www.dei-sales.com/store *and learn how to log on to these and other popular online courses:*

Sixteen Keys to Getting More Appointments

Sixteen proven techniques for getting more face-to-face meetings with prospects.

Using Questions to Accelerate Sales

Learn about the critical questions that will move relationships forward, speed up your sales cycle, and put money in your pocket.

Seven "Make It Happen" Questions You're Not Asking

This course includes the world's simplest—and most effective—closing technique.

The Monday Morning Meeting:
A Manager's Guide to Increasing Sales

Learn to ask the questions that will boost your team's performance dramatically!

Telesales

The D.E.I. *Telesales* workshop shows both inbound and outbound telesales professionals how to open the conversation, build rapport, gather information more effectively, customize the recommendation, and close more sales.

Thousands of companies worldwide have successfully implemented the principles in the *Telesales* workshop, including **Aetna, Intek/Sony, Nature America, Port, Inc., Reed Elsevier, Sprint,** and **Boise Office Solutions.**

As a direct result of the *Telesales* workshop, D.E.I. clients have found they better qualify their prospects and improve their closing ratios—in some cases by as much as **20 percent.**

To learn more about this live training program, call us at (800) 224-2140, or visit *www.dei-sales.com.*